THE LEEK &
MANIFOLD VALLEY
LIGHT RAILWAY

THE LEEK &
MANIFOLD VALLEY
LIGHT RAILWAY

KEITH TURNER

The
History
Press

Frontispiece: The official seal of the L&MVLR Co., designed by Sir Thomas Wardle, featuring Thor's Cave. The NSR's 'Staffordshire knot' emblem is included bottom right – though in a very insignificant size!

First published in 2005 by Tempus Publsihing

Reprinted with revisions in 2010 by
The History Press
The Mill, Brimscombe Port,
Stroud, Gloucestershire, GL5 2QG
www.thehistorypress.co.uk

Reprinted 2013

British Library Cataloguing in Publication Data.
A catalogue record for this book is available from the British Library.

ISBN 978 0 7524 2791 1

Typesetting and origination by
Tempus Publishing Limited.
Printed in Great Britain.

Contents

Preface

It is some thirty years since I first wrote an account of the Manifold Valley and its railway, and I am delighted to have been given the opportunity to bring the story up to date – again as an evocation of the railway in words and pictures, rather than a full-length technical or commercial history. During those intervening two decades the valley has, thankfully, changed but little and remains as delightful as ever. One major alteration though is immediately obvious to visitors: the refurbishment of the former station building at Hulme End and its reopening as an information centre. Long may it continue in its new role, once more serving faithfully its secret valley. And long may it embody the spirit of its little railway.

Keith Turner

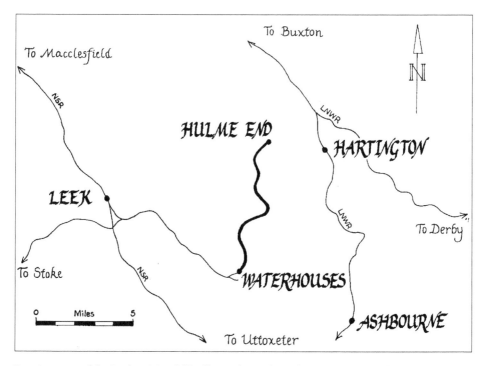

Location map of the Leek & Manifold Valley Light Railway, showing its relationship to the surrounding standard gauge lines.

Introduction

The valleys of the Manifold and its tributary, the Hamps, are, in point of beauty, among the most precious possessions of Staffordshire. They differ in character from the other moorland dales in being, generally speaking, less thickly wooded, less rocky and less steep-sided, and, in a word, more homely, but nevertheless they contain at certain spots rock scenery which in grandeur perhaps surpasses anything of the sort in the other dales, and their bare hill scenery has its own attraction.
Charles Masefield, *Staffordshire*, 1910

There is neither road nor footpath down the whole length of Manifold Valley, though these occur here and there. But the little railway threads its inmost recesses in a delightfully casual way, playing hide and seek with the cliffs and the waters, and the cars are built to make the best of the views in all directions.
Thomas L. Tudor, *The High Peak to Sherwood*, 1926

This book is the story in words and pictures of that little railway of the Manifold Valley. It is a railway I never knew personally, being of a much later generation. Indeed, more than seventy years have passed since the last engine steamed its unhurried way down the line – but its memory stubbornly refuses to fade. Each year countless thousands still thread those inmost recesses, only this time on foot and bicycle, for a footpath now plays hide-and-seek with the cliffs and the waters, and the casual little trains run only in the imagination.

Weags Bridge & Grindon Station.

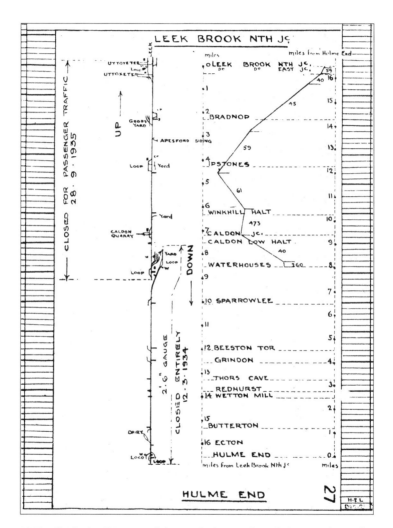

LMS official Line Diagram of the standard gauge branch from Leek Brook Junction to Waterhouses, and the narrow gauge Manifold from Waterhouses to Hulme End.

one
Conception

The Manifold Valley

The narrow gauge railways of Britain have seemingly had the gift of choosing some of the country's most beautiful scenery through which to run: the wilds of North Wales, the charms of Exmoor, the gentle peace of rural Suffolk to name but some. The Leek & Manifold Valley Light Railway (always familiarly known simply as 'the Manifold') was no exception to this rule, running for eight winding miles through the valleys of the River Manifold and its tributary, the Hamps. Situated in the north-east corner of Staffordshire and the south-west corner of the Peak District National Park, where the one spills over into the other, and overshadowed by its more famous neighbours, the Manifold Valley possesses a scenic grandeur all of its own. Never as well known as the nearby Dovedale and literally off the beaten track until the 1930s, it has never boasted a road running its full length and it was in fact to make the valley more accessible that the idea of the light railway was first mooted.

Lying roughly north-south on beds of millstone grit and limestone, the valleys of the Manifold and the Hamps cut through an area with few inhabitants and little obvious economic prosperity. There is some quarrying, and there was once some metal ore mining as well; agriculturally the land is poor, except when used for the raising of cattle and the production of milk, and the latter product was envisaged as providing the bulk of the projected railway's freight traffic while the passenger service, it was hoped, would bring in the day-trippers from the neighbouring urban areas of the Potteries, Derbyshire, and southern Lancashire and Yorkshire. This then was the great idea and it is to the credit of this predominantly rural corner of England that there could be found locally enough men of vision to back the dream with hard cash.

The Idea

Before 1896, in order to construct a railway for public traffic across other people's land, a great deal of money had to be spent on promoting a Bill through Parliament to secure the necessary powers to build such a line. Even then, there was no guarantee that such a Bill would overcome the inevitable opposition of hostile landowners, and of vested interests such as rival railway companies, and become an Act. In 1896, however, the Light Railways Act was passed by Parliament and, although several years too late when viewed in retrospect, it was to have an important effect upon the future railway map of Britain for it enabled railways to be promoted, constructed and worked with the minimum of expense. This was achieved by awarding a scheme not an Act of Parliament but a Light Railway Order (LRO), under which a standard or narrow gauge line could be authorised by the government's Light Railway Commissioners and be constructed to far less stringent standards than those required for other railways. Obviously, such a basic, light-weight railway could not be operated in main line fashion and certain restrictions on speed and working had to be observed. In addition, construction grants could be made available to deserving cases and, in many instances, the whole procedure proved an extremely sensible way of opening up rural areas hitherto untapped by conventional branch lines.

The Light Railways Act gave rise to a great many schemes that reached various stages of discussion and planning, in different parts of the country, before coming to nothing; the area around the north Staffordshire market town of Leek was no exception as several interested parties cast their eyes on the thriving local dairy industry, the output from which they believed could be fed profitably, by rail, into the national railway network. Another possibility given serious consideration was the construction of an electric tramway: the 1890s and 1900s saw them springing up all over central England, either as completely new lines or as conversions of older horse- or steam-worked systems (and, indeed, often constructed under the provisions of the Light Railways Act). To the south-east of the Manifold Valley, for example, the Midland Railway (MR) opened a 10-mile-long tramway between Burton-upon-Trent and Ashby-de-la-Zouch in 1903 while, even closer to the south-west, the Potteries Electric Traction Co. Ltd was busy constructing a comprehensive inter-urban system linking the towns and villages around Stoke-upon-Trent. It is not too fanciful to suppose that, had events taken only a slightly different course, an electric tramway rather than a steam railway might have served the Manifold Valley, doing a thriving trade carrying day-trippers and milk churns in exactly the same way as the electric Kinver Light Railway (opened 1901) did at the opposite end of the county.

Serious consideration of a railway in the Manifold Valley began even while the Light Railways Act was still being debated in Parliament, the ball being set rolling by the Reverend William Beresford, Vicar of St Luke's church in Leek, in an address on 4 November 1895. Letters to the press followed, accompanied by, and feeding, the inevitable local gossip and speculation, culminating in a public meeting in the town on 27 May 1896. One of the principal reasons for the concern shown in the area was that the London & North Western Railway (LNWR) was

---

THE LIGHT RAILWAYS ACT, 1896.

LEEK, CALDON LOW AND HARTINGTON LIGHT RAILWAYS.

ORDER OF THE LIGHT RAILWAY COMMISSIONERS

Authorising the construction of Light Railways in the County of Stafford from Cheddleton Junction on the North Stafford-shire Railway to Caldon Low and Hulme End.

The introduction to the 1898 Light Railway Order authorising the construction of both the NSR's standard gauge Waterhouses branch and the narrow gauge Leek & Manifold Valley Light Railway.

at that time constructing a branch from Buxton to Ashbourne – a branch which, it was feared, would take passengers and produce from the Manifold Valley to those two towns in preference to Leek. The resolution of the meeting – which had been called by Colonel Charles Bill, the local Member of Parliament – was that a committee be set up to promote a light railway linking Leek with the Manifold Valley. Bill was thereupon appointed Chairman of the Leek Light Railways Committee.

The Committee took the view that it would be better to co-operate with a major railway company, rather than go it alone, and so secured the interest of the LNWR's great rival in the region, the North Staffordshire Railway (NSR). The story of the time was that W.S. Watson, of Leek Rural District Council, invited the directors of the NSR to a 'good luncheon' at his house on market day, then took them for a drive along the road to Ashbourne. So impressed were they by the volume of traffic they saw heading for Leek that they promised immediately to build a standard gauge line connecting Leek to Waterhouses, from where a narrow gauge line would proceed up the Manifold Valley. True story or not – the fact that Bill was a director of the NSR perhaps lent more weight to the project's chances – what was fixed upon was a decidedly unusual, if not unique, arrangement whereby two separate lines would be built, one of standard and one of narrow gauge, by two different companies, all under the one LRO!

The application to the Light Railway Commission was made jointly by Bill and the NSR in May 1897; it was for a steam railway in two parts, one of which would be laid to a gauge of 4ft 8½in and the other to 3ft 6in, totalling approximately 17¼ miles in length and costing the estimated – and implausibly precise – sum of £144,300 6s 3d (£144,300.31). The Commission held its public enquiry into the application, in the normal course of events, on Tuesday 12 October at Leek and, despite appearances by two solicitors representing objectors, approved both it and the promotors' change of proposal to 2ft 6in for the narrow gauge section. (The reduction in gauge effected an estimated saving of £15,819 though the new choice of gauge was a curious one, 2ft 6in being virtually unheard of for a railway in Britain. A possible explanation is advanced later.) The draft Order was submitted to the Board of Trade on 21 July of the following year and its confirmation eagerly awaited.

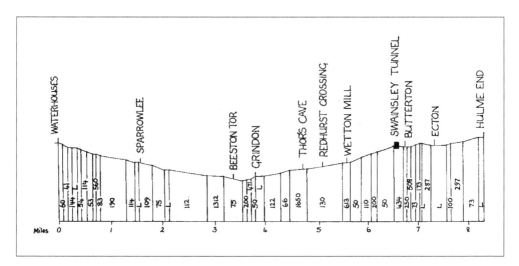

Gradient profile of the Manifold line, showing clearly how the railway descends gradually beside the River Hamps to its meeting with the River Manifold near Beeston Tor, then climbs slowly to the head of the latter's valley.

The Light Railway Order

The LRO was approved by the Board of Trade on 6 March 1899 as the Leek, Caldon Low & Hartington Light Railways Order 1898, empowering the construction of four sections of railway in all. The first three – all linked – were to be of standard gauge, forming a 9½-mile line running eastwards from a junction with the Churnet Valley line at Leek Brook, near Longsdon, to the village of Waterhouses with a half-mile branch south to the limestone quarries at Caldon Low; all three were to be constructed and worked by the NSR. The fourth section authorised was the narrow gauge Manifold line which the NSR, in the words of the LRO, 'have agreed to construct and work in perpetuity' for the Leek & Manifold Valley Light Railway Co.

The Manifold railway itself was to run for 8 miles and 8 chains (8 miles 176yd) from Waterhouses, in the parish of Caldon, to Hulme End, in the parish of Warslow and Elkstone. It was to be steam-operated with a gauge of 2ft 6in, and the time allowed for completion of the work was five years. Special provisions relating to the actual construction of the line were laid down as follows: Weight limit – 8 tons per axle. Rails – to be at least 35lb per yard, whilst on curves of less than three chains (198ft) radius, checkrails had to be provided. Turntables – 'No turntables need be provided'. Platforms – again, not needed if 'all carriages in use on the railway for the conveyance of passengers are constructed with proper and convenient means of access to and from' the ground. And finally – 'There shall be no obligation on the Company to provide shelter or conveniences at any station or stopping place.'

The Company referred to was the Leek & Manifold Valley Light Railway Co., which was itself incorporated by the LRO with a capital of £15,000 in £1 shares (in addition to any forthcoming Treasury grant). The first directors named in the LRO were Bill, Professor John Prince Sheldon, Sir Thomas Wardle, Frank Drewry, Arthur John Hambleton, John Brearley, Andrew Morton, Dr Alfred Hall and John Hall (nine was in fact the maximum number of directors permitted). All were local men and all, with the exception of Alfred Hall, were JPs. In addition, Hambleton was Chairman of the Leek Rural District Council, Morton was Chairman of the Leek Urban District Council and Professor Sheldon was Chairman of the Leek Board of Guardians – strong evidence of the depth of local support for the railway. Company Secretary was Edward Challinor of the Leek firm of Challinors & Shaw, solicitors to the railway company.

Railways authorised.

10. Subject to the provisions of this Order the Railway Company may make and maintain in the lines and according to the levels shown on the Plan and Section the railways hereinafter described with all proper and sufficient rails sidings junctions turntables bridges viaducts stations approaches roads yards buildings and other works and conveniences connected therewith. **Power to make railways.**

The railways hereinbefore referred to and authorised by this Order are :—

A Railway (No. 1) 8 miles 1 furlong 1·49 chains or thereabouts in length commencing in the parish of Longsdon by a junction with the Churnet Valley Line of the Railway Company and terminating in the parish of Caldon in a field numbered 205 on the 1-2500 Ordnance Map of that parish :

A Railway (No. 2) 4 furlongs 8·50 chains or thereabouts in length commencing in the said parish of Caldon by a junction with Railway (No. 1) at the termination thereof and terminating in the parish of Caldon in the field numbered 326 on the 1-2500 Ordnance Map of that parish :

A Railway (No. 3) 1 mile 1 furlong 9·80 chains or thereabouts in length commencing in the said parish of Caldon by a junction with the said Railway (No. 1) and terminating in the said parish of Caldon in a field numbered 331 on the 1-2500 Ordnance Map of that parish :

And subject to the like provisions the Company may make and maintain in the lines and according to the levels shown on the Plan and Section the railway hereinafter described with all proper and sufficient rails sidings junctions turntables bridges viaducts stations approaches roads yards buildings and other works and conveniences connected therewith (that is to say) :—

A Railway (No. 4) 8 miles 8 chains or thereabouts in length commencing in the said parish of Caldon at the termination of Railway (No. 3) and terminating in the parish of Warslow and Elkstones in the field numbered 508 on the 1-2500 Ordnance Map of that parish.

11. Railways (No. 1) (No. 2) and (No. 3) shall be constructed on a gauge of four feet eight and a-half inches and Railway (No. 4) shall be constructed on a gauge of two feet six inches and the motive power shall be steam or such other motive power as the Board of Trade may approve. **Gauge of railways and motive power.**

The four sections of railway authorised – three standard and one narrow gauge – as detailed in the 1898 LRO.

The L&MVLR Co.

While the application for the LRO was still under consideration, the embryonic L&MVLR Co. issued 10,000 copies of its prospectus on 15 December 1898. This document announced that £15,000 of share capital would be raised in £1 shares, a grant of £10,000 would be forthcoming from the Treasury, and a loan of a similar amount would be secured from Staffordshire County Council, all to finance the narrow gauge section of the line.

The prospectus stated that the railway would be of 2ft 6in gauge and was to be worked by either steam or electricity (the possibility of an electric tramway being still left open at that time); the carriages were to be 'modelled on the Tram System' – a reference to a type of low carriage, with end platforms and open-plan seating, characteristic of British rural steam tramways. Local passenger traffic was estimated at 35,000 journeys a year and considerable goods traffic was envisaged, not only milk (an estimated 653,000 gallons a year) and other dairy produce, but also coal (4,000-6,000 tons a year) and local limestone, corn and other feeds, horses, cattle, and all manner of commodities. It was stated that the NSR would 'work and maintain in perpetuity the line, receiving 55 per cent of the gross returns of the railway'; estimated annual revenue was given as £2,496 of which £1,123 would go to the Company and the remainder to the NSR. It was also hoped that the opening of the railway would in turn lead to the reopening of the Ecton lead and copper mines at the northern end of the railway. The line's tourist potential was not overlooked either, and any revenue from this source – 'excursionists', in the parlance of the day – would be over and above the figures already quoted. Joseph Forsyth of Stoke (brother of James Curphey Forsyth, the NSR's former Engineer and General Manager) was engaged as Engineer to the venture.

As regards the actual operation of the railway, the NSR had indeed agreed to work the line – initially for ninety-nine years – in return for fifty-five per cent of the gross receipts. There was a condition attached though: the possibility of working the line by electricity was investigated by Thomas Parker of Wolverhampton and his report was adverse to the idea, which was perhaps just as well since the NSR had said that it would not work the railway if electricity was used until it had proved its worth over the first twelve months of operation.

The LRO secured and the L&MVLR Co. established, it was now time for a practical start and on Tuesday 3 October 1899 the traditional railway ceremony of 'cutting the first sod' was performed by the Duke of Devonshire at Waterhouses in the presence of the railway's promotors and an official NSR party. The latter personages had journeyed by special train from the company headquarters at Stoke to Froghall, then continued by way of the existing cable-worked 3ft 6in gauge mineral tramway to Caldon Low before finally reaching their destination by road. It may have been an inconvenient and circuitous route but it must have certainly have underlined in forceful fashion exactly what benefits would result from the construction of the planned standard gauge section of line: output from the Caldon Low quarries up to this date had been running at about 1,000 tons per day but new workings were needed, and a better way of removing the rock from them – hence the planned light railway branch.

The ceremony was scheduled for 1.00 p.m., to be followed by a public luncheon an hour later in a marquee on the field, tickets for which could be purchased for 2s 6d (12.5p). The Duke of Devonshire almost did not make it – his train from Buxton to Hartington (near Hulme End) broke down that morning and he had to be brought to Waterhouses not exactly as had been arranged! He cut two sods, one for the standard gauge line and one for the narrow gauge, using a silver and mahogany spade and wheelbarrow made locally especially for the occasion. Presented to the Duke after the ceremony, they reside in the ancestral home of Chatsworth House. According to the *Manchester City News* of 7 October the Duke, proposing a toast to the success of the whole venture, predicted that the railway would cost less than £4,000 per mile to construct – as opposed

Early days: the grand opening of the Manifold at Waterhouses on Wednesday 29 June 1904, complete with hospitality marquee. The banners on the greenery arches proclaim 'Success to the Chairman of the Light Railway Company' and 'Welcome to Earl Dartmouth'. *Courtesy Peter Treloar*

to an average of £5,000 for other railways – and that £5 per mile per week would be a satisfactory return. Presumably more than satisfactory was the repast laid on for the dignitaries and guests by E.J. Wooldridge of the Station Hotel, Rudyard, and the Swan Hotel, Leek. The dishes are worth listing in full, if only so a faint flavour of such occasions of a bygone age can still be enviously savoured more than a century later: Crayfish in Aspic; Saddle of Roast Lamb; Fore-Quarter of Roast Lamb; Roast Beef; Hunters' Beef; Ox Tongue; Galatine of Veal; Boar's Head; Roast Ducklings; Roast Chickens; Game Pie; Veal and Ham Pie; Lobster Salad; Chicken Salad; Charlotte Russe; Whipped Cream in Open Jelly; Lemon Sponge; Lemon Jelly; Trifle; Macédoine de Fruits; Grapes, Apples, Pears, Bananas, Oranges, etc. – and all partaken of to the strains of a selection of light classics, rounded-off by a rendition of *The Blue Danube*, performed by the band of the Leek Company of the 1st V.B. North Staffordshire Regiment. At 6.30 p.m. a public dance began.

E.R. Calthrop

Colonel George Boughey, one of the three Light Railway Commissioners at this time, had examined the specifications drawn up for the construction of the line, and the tenders submitted, and presented his report to the L&MVLR Co. directors on 17 October 1900. His report expressed some dissatisfaction with the specifications and recommended that an independent expert should be called in to reappraise the matter. The person suggested by Boughey was E. R. Calthrop MICE, MIMechE of 3 Crosby Square in London (and previously Liverpool) who, since 1892, had run a consulting practice advising on engineering matters; at that point in his career his speciality was

The original, temporary station at Waterhouses, again on the railway's opening day, with a crowd of onlookers on the right massed in the village's main street – the Ashbourne road – and a small party of officials by the train's leading locomotive, No.2 *J.B. Earle*. *Courtesy Peter Treloar*

LEEK, CALDON-LOW AND HARTINGTON
LIGHT RAILWAYS.

———

CUTTING OF THE FIRST SOD

BY

His Grace the Duke of Devonshire, K.G.,

On Tuesday, October 3rd, 1899,

AT ONE O'CLOCK.

🔲

PUBLIC   LUNCHEON,

IN THE MARQUEE ON FIELD,

AT 1-30 O'CLOCK.

TOAST LIST.

1.—THE QUEEN, THE PRINCE OF WALES, AND THE
REST OF THE ROYAL FAMILY –
Proposer—The Chairman (Sir Thomas Salt, Bart).

2.—SUCCESS TO THE LEEK, CALDON-LOW AND HART-
INGTON LIGHT RAILWAYS—
Proposer—His Grace the Duke of Devonshire, K.G.
Responder—C. Bill, Esq., M.P.

3.—HIS GRACE THE DUKE OF DEVONSHIRE, K.G.--
Proposer—The Chairman.

4.—LOCAL AUTHORITIES—
Proposer—Sir Thomas Wardle, F.G.S., F.C.S.
Responder—J. P. Sheldon, Esq., J.P.

5.—THE CHAIRMAN—
Proposer—Robert Pearce, Esq.

Above left: The programme cover for the cutting of the first sod ceremony – the one occasion inaugurating the construction of both standard and narrow gauge lines.

Above right: The list of official toasts from the cutting of the first sod programme. Such speeches, intended primarily to reassure and impress would-be investors, were very much an integral part of such occasions and were widely reported in the press.

light railways and his credentials in that area were impeccable. Born in 1857, Everard Richard Calthrop had worked briefly for Robert Stephenson & Co. before serving his apprenticeship with the LNWR at Crewe from 1874 to 1879. He had then moved to the Great Western Railway, rising to the position of Assistant Manager in that company's Carriage & Wagon Works. In 1882 he had been appointed Assistant Locomotive Superintendent on the Great Indian Peninsula Railway, so beginning a long involvement with the railways of the sub-continent (as well as with those of the West Indies, Egypt and Europe). In 1895 the Barsi Light Railway Co. was set up in India to put his light railway theories into practice and two years later opened its first section of 2ft 6in gauge line. The great showcase for Calthrop's ideas, the Barsi railway proved immensely successful – by 1927 the system had reached a total length of over 200 miles – and firmly established him as one of the leading figures in this field. It was this background that led him to be called into the Manifold project and, as will be seen, the railway was to become his English showcase.

As remarked earlier, the choice of a gauge of 2ft 6in for the Manifold was a curious one – 2ft, 2ft 3in or 3ft being the norm for public narrow gauge railways in the British Isles at that time – with its use confined to a handful of non-passenger lines; it seems highly likely that Colonel Boughey, knowing of Calthrop's achievements with this gauge, himself recommended it to the Manifold's promoters at the time of the enquiry into their LRO application.

In 1897 Calthrop wrote a paper, entitled *Light Railway Construction*, to be read to the Cleveland (Middlesbrough) Institution of Engineers. In it he set out his theories with regard to this subject, and backed them up with actual examples of permanent way, locomotives, carriages and wagons from the newly-opened Barsi Light Railway. Where apposite, practical parallels between his Indian and English lines are noted elsewhere in this account; below are some extracts from Calthrop's paper which serve to illustrate his philosophical approach to the whole matter of light railways, their construction and their operation. For example, in addition to achieving the cost benefits accruing naturally from the adoption of a narrow, rather than standard, gauge, Calthrop believed that…

…the fundamental idea of light railway construction is the elimination of every kind of expenditure which is non-essential to its efficiency as a means of transport, and the reduction of all permanent way, plant, and appliances to their simplest and most inexpensive forms… For light railway work I am against all ornamental and unnecessary expenditure, particularly as regards the erection of permanent buildings, for the accommodation of employees, on a scale of extravagance altogether above the kind of habitations in which they are accustomed to live, and also as regards lavish accommodation at stations before traffic requirements are thoroughly tested.

In my opinion the fact that it is essential to their financial success that narrow gauge light railways have to be built and worked on principles and guided by rules totally divergent from those in use on standard gauge railways is a very strong argument in favour of their independent administration. The whole bent and training of the rank and file of the staff of a standard gauge line is towards solidarity and lavish expenditure, and with the advent of heavier train loads and higher speed this tendency will become more and more pronounced. The metier of the light railway man is, on the other hand, to eliminate expenses, superfluity, and complexity in every shape and form, and to evolve a type of line on which efficiency of action is combined in every department with the greatest simplicity of equipment. To place the working of a narrow gauge line, on which such a policy is required, in the hands of a staff furnished, changed and controlled by an adjoining standard gauge railway, and to expect it to carry out a role totally opposed to all its previous traditions is not likely to produce the desired results, and, so far as I am aware, has never yet done so.

In the light of the subsequent relationship between the L&MVLR Co. and the NSR, these were prophetic words indeed.

A postcard view of the temporary station at Waterhouses, used as the Manifold's southern terminus until the shared standard gauge/narrow gauge station was completed.

Another postcard of the temporary station at Waterhouses, this time as seen from the road, with one of the Straker steam buses working a shuttle service to Leek. The notice on the right warns road users of the level crossing in the distance.

A postcard view of the Manifold's northern terminus at Hulme End. The pile of bricks on the right appears to mark the site of the locomotive's watering tower, suggesting that the occasion is a pre-opening trial. The locomotive is the railway's No.1 *E.R. Calthrop*.

Another postcard of *E.R. Calthrop* at Hulme End, again possibly photographed before the railway opened to the public. The gentleman in the trilby is J.B. Earle, the Manifold's resident engineer.

The Manifold's second locomotive, No.2, was named after J.B. Earle, and is seen here on a train at Hulme End. The occasion is possibly the railway's opening day, or very soon afterwards.

Between the two termini the railway's intermediate stations were much of a type, differing only in minor details of track layout and facilities. This postcard shows the newly-built Wetton Mill Station with its characteristic low platform, wooden name board, 'bungalow' waiting room and a pair of bench seats. From the right the tracks are: the running line, a passing loop, and a siding leading to (just visible) a stop block and raised standard gauge length.

The first, temporary station at Waterhouses again, showing clearly the line's tight curve down to the level crossing.

An F. Moore's Railway Photographs postcard of *Skylark*, one of the two contractor's locomotives employed during the construction of the railway, in post-Manifold days.

two
Birth

Calthrop Takes Over

History resounds with the repeated cry of 'What if?' and the history of the Manifold is no exception to such speculation, for early in December 1900 Forsyth died – apparently without having been paid for his surveying work for the line – and on the 19th of that month the L&MVLR Co. directors met to consider the appointment of his successor. At the same time they discussed Calthrop's report on the specifications of the railway in which he promised that substantial savings could be made in the construction costs. He was thereupon offered the position of Engineer, which he promptly accepted, and set about putting his personal stamp on the railway, subsequently producing a masterpiece of British narrow gauge engineering. It may not have been as spectacular a line as some of the Welsh narrow gauge railways, or its locomotives so innovative, but it was, nevertheless, a masterpiece of overall design in its own right, proving just how competent a narrow gauge railway could be. It is probably not an exaggeration to say that if it had been built a quarter of a century earlier, hot on the heels of the Festiniog Railway's pioneering demonstrations of the potential of the narrow gauge steam locomotive, then the whole British railway network might well have had a vastly different appearance. Alas, it was built too late: its capabilities were not unheeded, but they were simply not called for elsewhere.

Right from its opening, the Manifold was noted for the smooth running of its stock, this being largely due to its substantial permanent way which – literally – formed the base upon which Calthrop could put his other design ideas into practice. Ballasted with limestone excavated during the construction of the line (and also brought from the Duke of Devonshire's workings at Ecton) the 35lb per yard flat-bottomed rails (rolled in Belgium) were spiked and screwed, in 24ft lengths, to 5ft x 8in x 4½in timber sleepers. A special feature of this robust design was the use of bearing plates on each sleeper which tilted each rail inwards just under three degrees from the vertical so that the top surface provided as good a match as possible with the profile of the wheel tyres; the expectation was that the life of both wheels and rails would consequently be greatly prolonged. Its success in practice can be judged from the fact that the Manifold's rails, despite being of the minimum weight specified in the LRO (and some two-thirds the weight of those used elsewhere in Britain on comparable narrow gauge railways) never had to be replaced during the railway's entire life. This was not a chance outcome, for Calthrop's confidence in such light rails came from his experience with them on the Barsi Light Railway.

Construction

Construction did not begin until March 1902, the delay in getting work underway being caused by financial problems: a condition of the government grant was that the Company's shares had to be fully taken up by 1902 and, in order to meet this requirement, those left at the end of 1901 had had to be taken up by Bill (and the other directors) to enable the project to go forward.

The contract for the construction of the Manifold was awarded to Messrs Hutchinson & Co. of Skipton – the contractors for the three standard gauge sections of the 1898 LRO – who in turn sublet the actual work to Messrs Henry Lovatt & Co. Ltd of Wolverhampton. On the railway side, Calthrop's brother-in-law John B. Earle, himself an established engineer, was appointed Resident Engineer for the project; he was assisted by G.J.R. Gossling while E. Godfrey Brewer, Calthrop's Assistant Mechanical Engineer, supervised the construction of the rolling-stock. A period of ill-health in 1903 meant that Calthrop had to delegate much of his own work on the railway to this team of associates.

Even allowing for the late start, the actual construction of the railway took surprisingly long for an 8-mile line, despite track-laying progressing from two sites at once. One reason was a serious outbreak of smallpox in the workmen's lodging huts at Butterton, another was the high standard of permanent way engineering insisted upon by Calthrop, and the many bridges (and one tunnel) demanded by the route. Poor road access did not help matters either. Details of actual construction procedure are sketchy but one useful account that has survived is that of the North Staffordshire Field Club whose members travelled the line on Saturday 22 August 1903. Not all the track had been laid by then and their journey over the railway was consequently made in two stages: Swainsley to Beeston Tor and Sparrowlee to Waterhouses, and on both sections they rode in contractor's wagons hauled by a contractor's locomotive.

During 1903 tenders received for the rolling-stock were considered by the directors but there was then further delay whilst more acceptable quotations were secured. On 5 August the tender submitted by Kitson & Co. Ltd of the Airedale Foundry, Leeds, was approved, for two engines at £1,725 each. It was not the lowest tender submitted but on Calthrop's advice the bid was accepted, presumably because of his satisfaction with the Barsi Light Railway engines supplied by this firm. Four passenger carriages were ordered from the Electric Railway & Tramway Carriage Works Ltd of Preston, variants of a common design: two bogie brake composites at £992 each and two bogie thirds at £946 each, plus one set of spare parts for £67 16s (£67.80). Again, Calthrop's recommendation had been adopted, for he had argued for an open saloon design of coach as opposed to a standard compartment type. At the same time, the goods stock was ordered. (Full details of all the railway's rolling-stock are given in Chapter 5.)

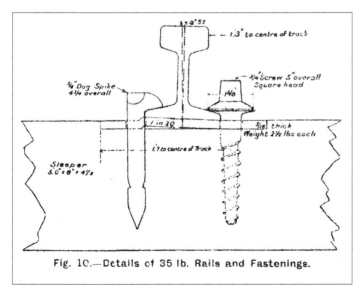

Fig. 10.—Details of 35 lb. Rails and Fastenings.

The Manifold's track fixings, showing Calthrop's adoption of tilted rails, as drawn for the *Tramway and Railway World*, 14 July 1904 article on the railway. The second rail was, of course, also angled inwards, as a mirror image of its companion.

In operation: the Manifold's permanent station at Waterhouses, shared with the NSR's branch from Leek, opened on 1 July 1905; this postcard view shows it shortly after that date. Note the many milk churns, and the loaded transporter wagon being shunted through the original goods shed. The evidence from later photographs and maps indicates that the station buildings were substantially altered and/or repositioned during their lifetime.

During its existence the NSR issued more than twenty sets of souvenir postcards, many of which featured the Manifold railway and the surrounding area. This monochrome example shows the railway passing End Farm, having just crossed the Ashbourne road and the River Hamps at Waterhouses.

The Manifold was more or less ready for traffic early in 1904, although the rolling-stock had not yet arrived. The prevailing mood in the Company was one of optimism throughout and on 25 February the board decided to press for an extension of the line to Longnor and Buxton (4 and 10 miles respectively in a north-westerly direction from the railway's northern terminus at Hulme End); the relevant county councils (Staffordshire and Derbyshire) were approached and agreed to lend support the proposal. Calthrop surveyed the route and his plans for the final approach to Buxton included a stretch of mixed-gauge track over the LNWR's route into the town! In hindsight, the extension would have made a lot of sense if it could have been built without visiting financial ruin upon the whole venture; as Gilbert J. Stoker pointed out in the *Railway Magazine* (September 1904), 'The importance of having an outlet at such an important centre of tourist and other traffic as Buxton can scarcely be over-rated.' At the same time the board settled some of the finer points of detail of the line as built, such as the names of the locomotives and the stations. All that was left was to decide the opening day: 23 May, Whit Monday.

In the final analysis the Manifold cost £35,944 to construct and, thanks to Calthrop, this figure was some £11,000 less than that estimated before he took control. When other costs such as engineers' fees (£4,275), locomotives (£3,450), legal charges, survey and promotional expenses, etc. (nearly £9,000) were added, the total came to £52,600 – not taking into consideration the cost of the carriages and wagons, half of which had not arrived by the opening day. Despite Calthrop's savings, this was twice what had been envisaged back in 1898 – the exorbitant prices demanded by landowners was a major factor – and to help make up the difference the original share capital of £15,000 was increased to £20,000 from 23 November (though the extra shares were not exactly snapped up); the Treasury similarly increased its grant from £10,000 to £17,500 and loaned a further £7,500 at 3 per cent while Staffordshire County Council lent £10,000 at 3½ per cent, thereby making a grand total of £55,000. The County Council loan was to be repaid in fifty annual instalments and was guaranteed by the Council being given the power to levy a rate (not exceeding 1*d* in the pound) from the villages along the line in the event of the railway not being able to make repayment.

The Route

Although from an operational point of view the Manifold commenced at Hulme End, it has always been more convenient and logical to regard it, for all other purposes, as beginning at Waterhouses. Here the NSR's standard gauge line from Leek came in from the west to terminate in a run-round loop by a single platform. A goods road and three sidings led back from here into the narrow gauge yard. The Manifold line came in from the east to occupy the northern side of the site and generally complemented its larger counterpart in layout (see accompanying map for details); the picture was completed by a main station building, built of wood to a typical NSR design, plus a signal box, a goods shed, and sundry other sheds and platelayers' huts. The Manifold had its own platform of course, complete with waiting room, set lower than that of the standard gauge and separated from it by a wooden fence. A little to the west of these platforms, both standard and narrow gauge lines crossed over a minor road on parallel stone bridges, between which a flight of steps ascended to the station. On the other side of the narrow gauge track, some 15ft below it at the bottom of a steep embankment, was the main Ashbourne road leading into the village, the whole station site being built on a terrace carved out of the hillside overlooking the roadway.

Leaving Waterhouses, the single line dropped on a 1 in 60 gradient before swinging northwards in order to cross the Ashbourne road approximately 330yd out from the station; the site of the railway's original temporary terminus was on the north side of the line immediately

An Edwardian coloured postcard, published by W. Shaw of Burslem, of the view south from Weags Bridge to the cliffs of Beeston Tor overlooking the confluence of the Rivers Hamps and Manifold. The small white rectangle at the foot of the Tor is the rear coach of a train in Beeston Tor Station. The child's message on the back of the card proclaims, 'I have seen the train on this picture. It is just like a toy train.'

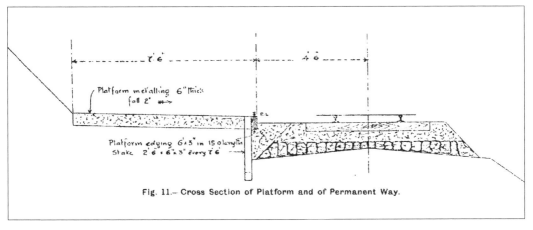

Fig. 11.– Cross Section of Platform and of Permanent Way.

Manifold permanent way and intermediate station cross-sections from the 1904 *Tramway and Railway World* article.

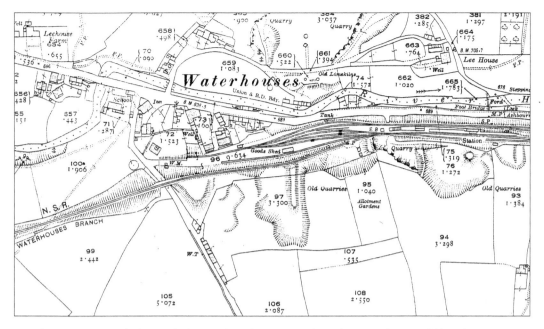

Waterhouses Station, with the standard gauge branch coming in from the west. The Manifold tracks occupy the north side of the platform and the goods yard. Short blocks have been added to indicate the end-on junctions of the two gauges in the sidings. This extract, and those following, are from the 1922 Ordnance Survey 25in to 1 mile series.

before this level crossing (the only major road crossing of any description on the railway). For journeys from Waterhouses the crossing gates were opened and shut either by the Waterhouses porter who bicycled down to do the necessary, or by the train's fireman and guard; on journeys from Hulme End the driver would whistle well in advance for the porter to set out to open and close the gates, so as to avoid halting the train on the stiff 1 in 41 gradient – the steepest on the railway – climbing towards Waterhouses.

Immediately beyond the road crossing came a bridge over the River Hamps as the railway continued its long curve northwards into its valley, the falling gradient easing gradually towards the first station, at Sparrowlee, 1½ miles from Waterhouses. Here there was an ornate wooden station sign and a bench seat for the benefit of those taking advantage of its meagre facilities – almost invariably day-trippers and picnickers, the station's original official and enticing designation being 'Sparrowlee for Waterfall'. Facing points led to a short siding/standard gauge section for transporter wagons (see Chapter 3); this siding was removed a few years before the line closed.

Sparrowlee was typical of the railway in that it never served more than a few scattered houses or farms in the immediate vicinity and, like the other intermediate 'stations', was in operating terms simply a request halt. Unless otherwise noted, each intermediate station described below had a similar name board and seat, and a single 'platform' constructed to the same Calthrop specifications: wooden edging, 4ft 6in from the track centre, was formed of 15ft lengths of 6in x 3in planks fastened to wooden stakes, behind which was a metalled area 7ft 6in wide rising from rail level at the front to 2in above it at the back.

The pattern of the railway was now set. Between its termini there were some two dozen short-span river bridges (and often the river had been diverted during construction to save

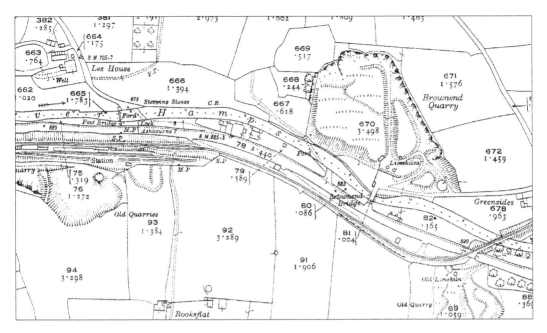

Waterhouses Station with the Manifold line falling away eastwards to the site of the original, temporary terminus just before the curve leading to the Ashbourne road crossing.

Thors Cave, Manifold Valley

A coloured postcard of a train at Thor's Cave Station, very soon after the railway opened – on the left is the first, short-lived refreshment hut, a companion building to the station bungalow. What appears to be a third structure further round the curve is in fact a haystack behind a gate.

building any more!) constructed of rolled steel joists, supported on stone abutments, carrying the running rails. The longest span was 42ft. (Steel instead of the originally-intended wood was used for the bridges, at the NSR's insistence, in order to save on maintenance costs.) There were also some two score bends, the sharpest of which had a radius of 4 chains (264ft), and it was these features that accounted for the following purple passage in a NSR publicity guide issued after the opening of the line:

This little but convenient light railway, by its startling, almost sensational, but absolutely safe insinuosities, reminds one of the zig-zags of the 'corkscrew' railway over the Semmering to Vienna, on which, according to a facetious engineer – the traveller can see the nape of his own neck, so continually winding is the line.

The next stop was at Beeston Tor (3½ miles), sited on a long curve, where the River Hamps flowed into the River Manifold, though this was not always obvious to summer visitors for the water often disappeared down swallet holes to follow an underground course for a while, leaving the pebbly beds completely dry, the province of the giant burdock (this behaviour of the Manifold and Hamps rivers is so bizarre that, in the words of Charles Masefield's 1910 *Staffordshire*, they 'are in their way natural curiosities through their strange habit of diving into subterranean channels... so numerous that up to the present all attempts to stop them with cement have signally failed.'). Although the station did not boast a siding, there was the usual seat and sign, plus a platelayers' hut and an old coach body – presumably of NSR origin – used as a waiting room. Nearby was a large wooden refreshment room operated by one of the Manifold's enterprising shareholders, a Mr Wood. This was for the benefit of day-trippers inspecting a cave, at the foot of the neighbouring hill from which the station took its name, reputed to have been the hermitage of one St Bertram. A Saxon hoard was discovered here in 1924. (Mr Wood, incidentally, was one of that select group who could claim to have travelled on both the first and last passenger trains over the railway.)

The railway now entered the most picturesque section of its route, winding as closely beside the Manifold as it had the Hamps (though crossing it rather less frequently) with the impressive bulk of the crowding limestone hills ever at hand. This was the lowest stretch of the railway, the line having fallen constantly (apart from the odd level section) all the way from Waterhouses. The next station was Grindon (4 miles), situated immediately north of the point where the railway crossed the Grindon to Wetton road; immediately to the east of the station the road crossed the River Manifold at Weags Bridge. Approached by an up gradient of 1 in 50 but sited on the level, the station comprised a shelter and a 'loop' which would have been a proper loop if not for the standard gauge track section in the middle of it. This provided goods facilities for the neighbourhood, and at the time of its construction an access track between here and Beeston Tor, on the eastern side of the railway, was laid in to allow local farmers to make use of them. (This was insisted upon by the local estate owner, hence its long-lasting nickname of 'Earl Cathcart's Road'.) The simple but attractive wooden shelters erected here and at several of the intermediate stations were known officially as 'bungalows' and were of great benefit to hikers – and others – waiting for a train in the rain; they were supplied at a cost of £40 each by the Portable Building Co. Ltd (who also provided the station name boards).

From Grindon the line now climbed virtually all the way, with the river, to Hulme End. Thor's Cave – officially 'Thor's Cave for Wetton' – was reached three quarters of a mile further on and here was a shelter (but no loop or siding) and, until 1917, a refreshment room; the original wooden building – like that at Beeston Tor, a Portable Building product – was replaced in 1905 (after it burnt down) by a larger, corrugated iron structure which in turn was sold in 1917 for £50 (with a rebate of £2.50 for cash!) and moved to Wetton to become the village reading

Thor's Cave, Manifold Valley, North Stafford Railway.

Above: Thor's Cave Station, on a card sent from Hanley to Cambridge in 1907: 'Fred & I were up in this district a week yesterday. It is very nice indeed.' Note the replacement refreshment room – and the simple conveniences added behind the bungalow! *Courtesy Jan Dobrzynski*

Right: The railway below Thor's Cave, on an anonymous black and white postcard. Posted on 7 August 1933, just seven months before the line closed, it carries the message, 'Today we are visiting the Manifold Valley which is very pretty... We came to here from Waterhouses on a little toy railway & we are going back on the same.' Presumably the card was printed many years earlier, for clearly visible on the right are the remains of the refreshment hut shown in the previous picture, burnt down in 1905.

THOR'S CAVE, MANIFOLD VALLEY.

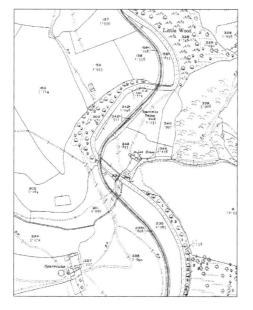
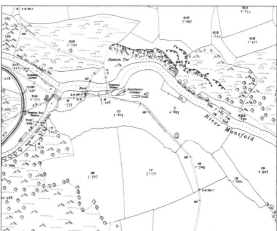

Above left: Sparrowlee Station, the first stopping place on the railway, with the goods siding leading to the standard gauge section on the other side of the running line from the platform.

Above right: Beeston Tor Station: no goods facilities but a footpath leading, by bridge over the River Hamps and by ford or stepping stones over the River Manifold, to the Tor itself.

room. Again, typical of the Manifold's intermediate stations, the village of Wetton it purported to serve was a mile or so away. Across the river was the eponymous cave with its gaping mouth, some 35ft high, set commandingly in the 300ft limestone cliff, and the stop was a popular picnic spot and starting point for a day's exploration – so much so that the station boasted two bench seats for waiting passengers! The cliff and cave mouth featured on the L&MVLR Co.'s official seal, designed in 1899 by Sir Thomas Wardle, and were reached by footpath across a bridge provided by the NSR. Tickets were issued by the County Council for entry to the cave.

At 5¼ miles came Redhurst Crossing – never a proper 'station' even by the Manifold's standards, but merely a 'halt' (though the difference on the Manifold was always academic) for the collection of milk by a convenient minor road crossing. Redhurst was in fact the only instance of a station – apart from the technical case of Waterhouses – being opened after the railway began service. The milk stage came first, in October 1907, followed by the passenger halt in July 1915, with another grounded standard gauge coach body brought in to serve as a waiting room.

Wetton Mill (again, at least a mile from Wetton Village) sat 5½ miles from Waterhouses and was nominally regarded as the halfway mark on the Manifold in operating terms, and in recognition of this fact was equipped with a proper passing loop as well as the more usual siding and standard gauge length. Since, however, the railway was only ever worked with one engine (or pair of engines) in steam, or with one train following another at a safe interval, it is believed this loop was never used as intended. This too was a well-frequented picnic spot – as indeed it is today – and offered children the added delight of a safe splash in the river. Facilities included the standard bungalow, and two seats.

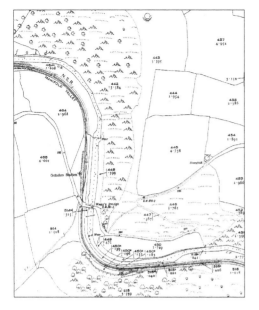
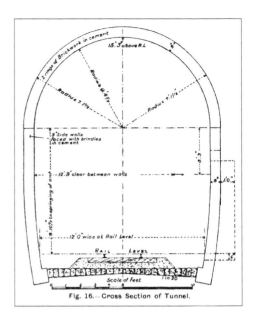

Fig. 16.—Cross Section of Tunnel.

Above left: Grindon Station, just to the north of the level crossing by Weags Bridge. Note the 'loop' with its central standard gauge section.

Above right: Swainsley Tunnel cross-section, again as drawn for the *Tramway and Railway World* of 14 July 1904.

From Grindon to Wetton Mill the railway had climbed relatively gently but now the gradient stiffened considerably to 1 in 50 for much of the way to Swainsley Tunnel, just before Butterton Station (6¾ miles) was reached. The straight tunnel, lined with two courses of brick and of generous clearance gauge at 12ft 9in wide and 15ft 3in from rail level to roof (to allow for the passage of the largest NSR wagon – a horse box – on a transporter), passed under part of the Swainsley estate. The limestone excavated from it was used as a foundation for the track bed in the vicinity. Curiously, widely differing figures were given from the first for the length of this tunnel: in 1904 for example the *Railway Magazine* gave it as 170yd whilst the journal *Engineering* opted for the more precise-sounding 167yd – both magazines basing their accounts of the line on facts and figures supplied by the Company. Major Druitt however (see below) officially recorded it earlier that year as 164yd.

Dating from 1867, Swainsley Hall was owned by Sir Thomas Wardle who, apart from his directorship of the L&MVLR Co., was a prominent local industrialist and an acquaintance of several members of the Pre-Raphaelite school of artists. Despite his connection with the railway, he insisted on the tunnel being built so that the line could not be seen from his residence – perhaps to avoid offending the artistic sensibilities of some of his house guests! Butterton station itself – originally known locally as 'Ecton Lea' – comprised the normal shelter and a set of trailing points leading to the usual standard gauge section, and occupied a short dip in the line's gradient profile. Sandwiched between the station and the northern portal of the tunnel was a short bridge spanning a tributary of the River Manifold, the Warslow Brook.

At Ecton (7¼ miles) the line dipped slightly again as the valley opened out and the trees became sparser. Here, during the eighteenth and early nineteenth centuries, there had been deep and extensive lead and copper workings under the hill across the river. These had provided

Wetton Mill Station, Manifold Valley, North Stafford Railway.

Although this card is captioned 'Wetton Mill Station', the station is actually some yards further to the left. Presumably the train – ready to departure for Waterhouses as soon as its crew stops posing for the camera – was halted here as it made for a far more scenic shot. The stream in the foreground is the Hoo Brook, about to join the River Manifold the other side of the railway.

a considerable portion of the Dukes of Devonshire's immense fortune, but by the time of the Manifold's coming they had been abandoned (an oft-repeated story was that in 1780 the 5th Duke built the Crescent at Buxton, at a cost of £120,000, out of just one year's mine profits). The hope was that the railway would revive the industry, but the ore in what had once been Britain's deepest mine – one shaft descended 1,400ft – was already worked out. The extensive spoil heaps, however, were utilised to feed a crusher during the construction of the railway, thus ensuring an endless supply of ballast stone at the bargain price of ¾d a ton – with the surplus being sold by the Company to local farmers as hardcore at 4d a ton! Officially entitled 'Ecton for Warslow', the original track layout appears to have been just the running line, as at Beeston Tor and Thor's Cave, with a full-length loop with a transporter siding running off it added in 1905; there was also a bungalow then erected on the other side of the line. A creamery was opened here, on the site of an old smelting house, in 1918 by F.W. Gilbert Ltd (later United Dairies) and a second siding, some 200yd long, was laid into the cheese factory. From then until its closure the creamery was the chief supplier of goods traffic on the Manifold, though in later years the nearby stone workings threatened literally to overshadow it; the latter, however, were entirely road-served.

Finally, the line meandered into Hulme End (8¼ miles from Waterhouses), where 'the railway and the finer portion of the valley alike terminate, the Manifold being comparatively a tame stream from this point upwards to its source near Flash' (Masefield). This northern terminus of the line, opposite the chapel on the western edge of the linear village, was originally known officially as 'Hulme End for Hartington', then later 'Hulme End for Sheen and Hartington' – Hartington, on the LNWR's line from Ashbourne to Buxton, being 2 miles and a 6d bus ride away! At the

By way of contrast, this is the Manifold as it appeared in 2002. Here at Waterhouses, this is the refurbished goods shed.

E.R. Calthrop heads south past Redhurst Crossing and over the river bridge. The coal wagon on the first transporter belongs to the Staffordshire concern of Robert Heath & Sons of Norton and Kidsgrove.

other end of the village, on the road to Hartington, the Waggon & Horses public house took the opportunity afforded by the arrival of the railway in Hulme End to change its name to the more progressive-sounding Light Railway Hotel. (In later years the hotel was a favourite retreat of the actor and film star Robert Donat when he wished to escape the glare of publicity.)

Because of the plan to extend the line to Buxton, the envisaged mid-way point of Hulme End was chosen to be the railway's headquarters; consequently the Manifold's engine and carriage sheds were located here, with the result that in later years it seemed positively eccentric to have sited them so far from the line's standard gauge connection.

The station layout was of a single platform with a loco run-round loop on one side, and two sidings both leading to standard gauge sections, each capable of holding ten or so wagons, on the other (the second standard gauge section was added eighteen months after the station opened, in response to a perceived need for it). The approach to the station was up a gradient of 1 in 73 although the actual terminus was on the level. Here was the railway's only crane, used for light repair work on the locomotives; major work had to be dealt with at Stoke or Crewe. Interestingly, the single-storey wooden station building, which cost £137 11s (£137.55) and proudly plated as another structure designed and erected by the Portable Building Co. Ltd of Fleetwood, Manchester, London and Johannesburg, was lit by electricity supplied by accumulators. At the end of day any steam pressure left in the locomotive in service was used to power a generator to recharge them. The water supply for the engines was pumped up to an overhead tank from a stream coming in from the west, the stream itself being used to drive an overshot wheel to work the pump.

The two-road engine shed was sited at the end of the run-round loop, with the two-road carriage shed located off the loop itself. Both were built by Isaac Dixon & Co. at a cost of £219 and £258 respectively. Other structures typical of a country railway terminus, besides the water tower, included a coaling stage, a weigh-bridge, assorted storage huts (including two formed from grounded carriage bodies for the storage of parcels and bicycles), and a number of local coal merchants' offices. Illumination was by oil lamps.

In contrast to the NSR's monochrome official postcards mentioned earlier, the coloured variety were far more attractive. This postcard, of the River Hamps near Waterhouses Station, was posted in 1917. *Courtesy Jan Dobrzynski*

A view of the track near Sparrowlee, with one of the railway's many river bridges in the middle distance. Note the checkrail in the foreground, a safety measure used on tight curves.

The halt at Redhurst Crossing in 1934 – the year the railway closed – with, from the left, the stage for milk churns, the name board and the 'waiting room'. *H.C. Casserley*

Another black and white NSR postcard, this time featuring a train heading south between Wetton Mill and Redhurst Crossing, with Darfur Crags looming over railway and river. This was one of the few sections of the railway – apart from at the termini – that came even close to a road.

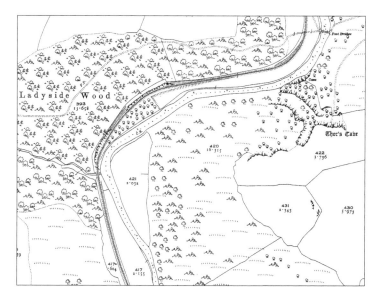

Thor's Cave, with its rail and footpath approaches. The actual station of that name was just a platform and shelter on the outside of the curve immediately beyond the northern edge of the map sheet.

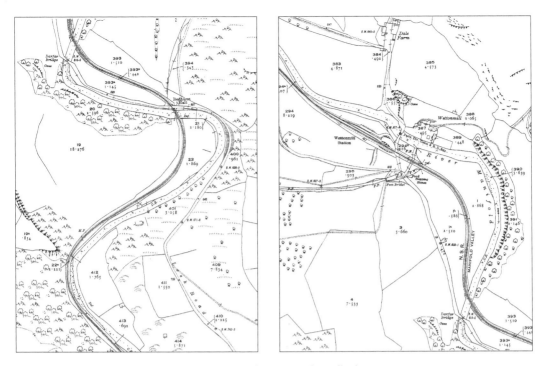

Above left: Redhurst Crossing: primarily a pick-up point for milk churns, not passengers.

Above right: Wetton Mill Station, with its road bridge over the river, and redundant passing loop.

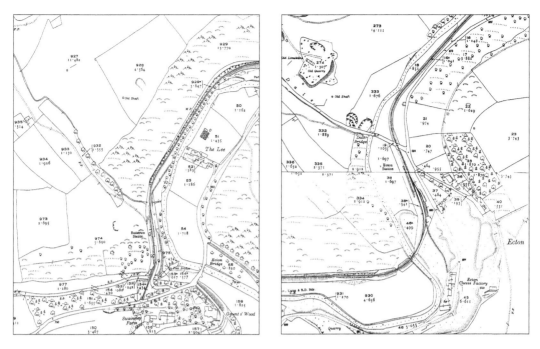

Above left: Butterton Station and the northern end of Swainsley Tunnel. Swainsley Hall is the large building bottom right.

Above right: Ecton Station in its final form, with a run-round loop and two sidings, the long one serving the new creamery.

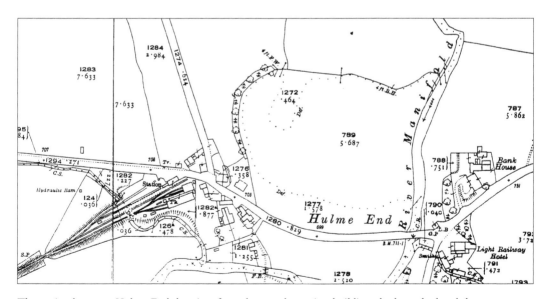

The station layout at Hulme End showing, from the top, the station building, the loco shed and the carriage shed. As today, the whole village comprises just a scattering of buildings, on a minor road, surrounded by fields.

Opening Day

As mentioned above, the intention was to open the railway on 23 May, Whit Monday 1904 but, since the line's two locomotives had only just arrived by then, the directors reluctantly took a cautious approach and put back the grand day to 27 June (also a Monday) so that proper running trials could be carried out. A second drawback was that only two of the ordered four coaches had arrived, whilst a further problem was the fact that the NSR had not yet completed its standard gauge line from Leek to Waterhouses, so plans were instead made for a steam bus service between those two places to be operated as a temporary measure until the branch opened. It would appear though that the branch was complete enough for the narrow gauge stock to be brought in over it to Waterhouses.

Prior to its opening, the narrow gauge railway underwent its statutory inspection by the Board of Trade, in the person of Major F. Druitt. His report, dated 23 June, commented extremely favourably on the design and construction of the railway, and passed it fit for passenger traffic. Among the details he noted of the line, the following deserve mention here:

Sharpest curve:	4 chains (88yd) radius
Deepest cutting:	15ft
Highest embankment:	17ft
Underbridges:	24
Longest bridge span:	40ft
Public road level crossings:	6

Interestingly, Druitt recorded the steepest gradient on the railway as being 1 in 50 – a figure appreciably different from other accounts of the time. Was it possible that perhaps he was purposefully misled over the true state of affairs, given that the location of this slope was by a major road crossing on the approach to Waterhouses station?

On the designated opening day, various groups of officials, guests, reporters and sightseers converged on the little village of Waterhouses, assembling at a temporary terminus on the Waterhouses Station side of the Ashbourne road crossing. The main party from Stoke (including W.D. Phillips the NSR's General Manager, his assistant and his Chief Engineer, plus assorted journalists) left that town at 9.45 a.m. and travelled by special train over the NSR as far as Cheddleton, thence over the branch to Waterhouses where decorations – especially grand floral arches – were much in evidence and the Caldon Low Brass Band in attendance. A general holiday had been declared and flags, bunting and banners flew from many of the houses, with one banner in particular – 'Hurry up, North Stafford' – exhorting the NSR to get on with its line from Leek! From the opposite direction came a second train: steaming in from Hulme End was the Manifold train made up of engines No.1 *E.R. Calthrop* and No.2 *J.B. Earle*, two coaches and two open wagons. The latter had been fitted with temporary seats for the great occasion and were used for the conveyance of, among others, members of the press. In the words of the *Railway Magazine* correspondent, Gilbert J. Stoker, 'from personal experience we can testify that they ran as smoothly as passenger carriages'.

The smooth running of all the stock was one of the features of the line which drew favourable comment in the railway and engineering press right from the very beginning to the very end of its life; not so favourable was the criticism voiced in some quarters that the names of the locomotives reflected an unhealthy degree of egotism on the part of their namesakes. It was suggested that it would have been more far more fitting to have named them after local features, such as the Manifold and the Hamps, as was the practice on other comparable lines (the Lynton

& Barnstaple Railway, for example, named its engines after Devon rivers and the Southwold Railway, in Suffolk, after the villages it served). This, though, was not always the case: for example, both the Welshpool & Llanfair Light Railway and the Glyn Valley Tramway, on the Welsh border, named their engines after personages connected with those lines.

The Earl of Dartmouth, Lord Lieutenant of Staffordshire, officially – and briefly – declared the line open at 11.20 a.m. and three minutes later the inaugural train pulled slowly out of the temporary station (the locomotives having in the meantime run round their train in the Waterhouses goods yard loop). The journey was leisurely, enabling guests, officials, reporters and other passengers – some 200 in total – to enjoy the scenery, with Hulme End being reached at 11.57 a.m. Here, everyone alighted to inspect the station, sheds and rolling-stock, and to pose stiffly for the obligatory photographs. In the yard, Brewer laid on a special demonstration of one of the transporter wagons (possibly the only one to have arrived). This naturally received a great deal of attention from members of the press, all of whom appear to have reported on it with enthusiasm, and it was attached to the train for the slightly speedier return trip (which was accomplished in twenty-three minutes).

As was traditional on such occasions of the age, the festivities, speeches and mutual congratulations now began, in a marquee in the field by the village Post Office. Catering this time was by Mr W. Bentley of the Crown Hotel, Waterhouses, with a spread only slightly less splendid than that laid on when the first sod was cut. Among those present at the celebratory luncheon were Lord Dartmouth (who proposed 'Success to the Light Railway'), the Manifold directors and officials (the former having had to buy their own tickets for the run over the line!), representatives of the NSR and the various contractors and suppliers to the line, together with several other railway company officials including, from India, the General Traffic Manager of the Southern Mahratta Railway. Representing the British narrow gauge scene were J.R. Dix, General Manager of the Corris Railway in mid-Wales, and Sir Arthur Heywood, the famous advocate of minimum gauge lines. Professor Sheldon proposed the toast of 'The Engineers and Contractors' and with his reply Calthrop brought the official side of the proceedings to a close. The *Tramway and Railway World* summed up the mood of the day in its article of 14 July:

This light railway, which taps the very centre of the district, will waken it to new life, and will reveal its possibilities to the inhabitants, to the tourist, and to all those interested in the development of our native resources...

That there are many openings, not only in foreign parts, but also in Great Britain, for similar lines is incontestable. It is to be hoped that the Leek & Manifold Valley Light Railway will prove to be the pioneer of many similar undertakings.

With its universally favourable coverage of the railway's design, construction and opening, the feelings of the technical press towards the promoters were, in turn, captured perfectly by Gilbert Stoker in his article in the *Railway Magazine* (see above):

We trust that the aspirations of those who have given much time and thought, and contributed their money, to the scheme, will be realised, and that the 'little railway' will be a big success in every respect.

Among the itemised expenditure made that day were the sums of £5 for the rent of the field, £40 5s (£40.25) to Bentley for supplying 322 cold lunches at 2s 6d (12.5p) a time, £2 5s (£2.25) spent on drinks for the police and railway workers – and £4 spent on wine for the gentlemen of the press. As regards the value placed on favourable publicity, and the surest way to procure it, it would appear that some things have never changed!

Wetton Mill Station, looking away from the road bridge over the river, with a train of three coaches in original yellow livery. The mid-point of the railway was marked by a passing loop, though this was never used as intended. *Courtesy Peter Treloar*

The Steam Buses

Although the Manifold was now finally in business, its problems were not yet over. Due to persistent and heavy rain, the construction of the standard gauge branch between Cheddleton Junction and Waterhouses was held up for nearly a year. Cutting walls collapsed and, on one occasion, a whole embankment slumped away. Fully aware that the whole point of the Manifold would be lost if it did not link up with the rest of its system, the NSR purchased a pair of Bristol-built Straker steam buses to operate a temporary connecting service between Waterhouses, Leek and Ashbourne. Each was coke-fired (to avoid the smoke-emission problem) and powered by a 35hp engine with two horizontal cylinders. Chain-driven to the rear axle, they weighed just under three tons each. Both were painted in NSR carriage livery of madder-lake with yellow lining and cream upper bodywork, and were inscribed: LEEK, WATERHOUSES & HULME END. Their registration numbers were E192 and E223.

Trials of the buses were held in the May and June of 1904 and, after Parliamentary permission for their use in public service was given on 24 June, it is believed they entered service on the Manifold's opening day – or so it was reported in the press, although posters (printed in advance) gave a commencement date of 29 June. It seems that they were an immediate success with the public, though they were certainly not so popular in other quarters for the local authorities complained that they broke up the roads, while shopkeepers bemoaned the fact that the vibration set up by their passing shook their window displays to pieces!

Journey time for a bus over the eight miles between Leek and Waterhouses was exactly one hour, with a single fare of 8d (3.5p) charged. Seating was provided for twenty-two, with some standing room, and, when space was at a premium, preference was given to those who were continuing their journey on the Manifold (on one occasion no less than forty-two passengers were reported to have crammed themselves into one of the buses!). Although running trials were conducted as far as Ashbourne, regular workings were confined to the Leek-Waterhouses route. Despite the legend on the side, they did not venture to Hulme End, this presumably being a reference to the Manifold's part of the overall service.

Judged by later standards, the buses were unreliable, one even breaking down on the very first day, much to the embarrassment of the NSR! Moreover, with iron tyres and bone-shaking motion, they were decidedly uncomfortable machines in which to travel and soon earned the nicknames 'Earthquake 1' and 'Earthquake 2' (even if regarded by passengers as preferable to existing alternatives). In June 1905, however, the standard gauge line from Cheddleton was opened to passengers as far as Ipstones and buses from Waterhouses terminated here, rather than at Leek, until services to Waterhouses by rail finally began on 1 July that year. The two buses were thereupon taken out of service and transferred by the NSR to Stoke for use as excursion vehicles in the Potteries area. They were later sold there to a Mr Leveson Wedgwood of the North Road Boiler Works and converted into furniture removal vans.

Poster advertising the temporary steam bus service linking Waterhouses with Leek until the standard gauge branch opened. Note that though a starting date of 29 June 1904 is announced, the service actually began two days earlier.

three
Life

Under the NSR

The Manifold had opened before it was fully finished, and the first few years of its life were spent on the tidying-up of such loose ends that remained – for example the provision of earth-closet lavatories at the stations – and the completion of the permanent station at Waterhouses, which was brought into use in 1905 when the standard gauge branch finally opened on 1 July that year. In the words of Charles Masefield (1910) again:

On the whole, there is little to regret in the advent of the railway. From the utilitarian standpoint it has placed a once remote pastoral district within reach of a market for its milk, and even the most conservative lover of nature undefiled is bound to admit that the making of the line has done wonderfully little to desecrate the scenery.

As regards the envisaged northwards extension to Buxton, the NSR refused to consider a line progressing beyond Longnor and the idea was consequently dropped. Opposition to the scheme from landowners and the LNWR ensured that it was never resurrected. The dispute was symptomatic of a growing rift between the Manifold and the larger company, the cause of which was largely financial: the NSR soon realised that whatever else the Manifold was, it was certainly not a money-spinner, and petty rows broke out between the two companies over such details as how many trains should be run in the winter. By 1908 these squabbles had so annoyed the Manifold's directors that they were considering whether to ask the NSR to take over the line entirely, or to take legal action against it for its handling of the line's financial affairs. In the event, nothing came of these deliberations, other than a new agreement made shortly after the railway's opening to the effect that the L&MVLR Co.'s forty-five per cent of the railway's gross receipts should not be subject to any deduction of working expenses.

It would appear that, from the outset, the NSR adopted a decidedly ambivalent attitude towards the Manifold. On the one hand, it encouraged the influx of 'excursionists' by advertising the attractions of this 'Toy Railway' – but on the other, it actively tried to discourage passengers at peak times by offering only a limited service (and passenger capacity). Goods traffic was also discouraged by the simple means of charging higher rates for carriage than its competitors, much to the annoyance of the Manifold's directors and shareholders. A cynical conclusion would be that the NSR was interested only in its standard gauge branch to Waterhouses, and the Caldon Low traffic, but, since the Manifold had come as part of the package, it was grudgingly allowed to eke out a hand-to-mouth-existence.

Such differences between the two companies would simply have served to reinforce Calthrop's views on the subject, cited earlier. On the specific question of the Buxton extension, another quote from his 1897 paper is especially apposite:

LEEK and HULME END.—North Staffordshire.

Miles		Week Days								Sundays
		mrn		mrn		aft		aft	aft	aft
	Leek ....dep.	8 50	Wednesdays only.	1055	Saturdays only.	1 50	Wednesdays only	2 25	4 45	5 15
3½	Bradnop	8 1		11 6		2 1		2 36	4 56	5 26
5½	Ipstones ¶	8 8		1118		2 8		2 43	5 3	5 33
9½	Waterhouses .... arr.	9 20		1125		2 20		2 55	5 15	5 45
	dep.	9 35		1130		2 30		3 5	5 20	6 15
11½	Sparrowlee	9 40		1135		2 35		3 10	5 25	6 20
13½	Beeston Tor	9 49		1144		2 44		3 19	5 34	6 29
13¾	Grindon †	9 52		1147		2 47		3 22	5 37	6 32
14½	Thor's Cave *	9 57		1152		2 52		3 27	5 42	6 37
15½	Wetton Mill	10 1		1156		2 56		3 31	5 46	6 41
16½	Butterton	10 8		12 3		3 3		3 38	5 53	6 48
17	Ecton, for Warslow	1011		12 6		3 6		3 41	5 56	6 51
18	Hulme End † ....arr.	1015		1210		3 10		3 45	6 0	6 55

Miles		Week Days									Sundays
		mrn	mrn		mrn		aft		aft	aft	aft
	Hulme End ....dep.	3 el.	8 40	Wednesdays only.	1035	Saturdays only.	1 25	Wednesdays only.	2 0	4 25	5 0
1	Ecton, for Warslow	....	8 44		1039		1 29		2 4	4 29	5 4
1½	Butterton	....	8 47		1042		1 32		2 7	4 32	5 7
2¼	Wetton Mill	....	8 54		1049		1 39		2 14	4 39	5 14
3½	Thor's Cave *	....	8 58		1053		1 43		2 18	4 43	5 18
4¼	Grindon	....	9 3		1058		1 48		2 23	4 48	5 21
4¾	Beeston Tor	....	9 6		11 1		1 51		2 26	4 51	5 26
6½	Sparrowlee	....	9 15		1110		2 0		2 35	5 0	5 35
8½	Waterhouses ¶ .... arr.	....	9 20		1115		2 5		2 40	5 5	5 40
	dep.	....	9 30		1135		2 30		3 10	5 25	6 10
12½	Ipstones	6 50	9 44		1149		2 44		3 24	5 39	6 24
14½	Bradnop	7 0	9 50		1155		2 50		3 30	5 45	6 30
18	Leek 578, 574 ....arr.	7 10	10 0		12 5		3 0		3 40	5 55	6 40

NOTES.

* Station for Wetton.

† Station for Sheen (1¼ miles) and Hartington 1½ miles).

¶ "Halts" at Winkhill and Caldon Low, between Ipstones and Waterhouses.

Waterhouse Tickets are available at Caldon Low.

Manifold timetable, as published (above) in *Bradshaw's Monthly Railway Guide* for January 1915 and (below) for January 1923. The Sunday service remains fixed at one train each though the different weekday services have been standardised. Note that in both cases Leek–Hulme End is presented as though all one branch, with no mention of any change of train – or gauge – at Waterhouses!

LEEK, WATERHOUSES, and HULME END.—North Staffordshire.
☞ Third class only between Leek and Waterhouses.

Miles		Week Days				Suns.
		mrn	aft		aft	aft
	Leek ....dep.	9 5	1 55	Saturdays. Wednesdays and	4 35	3 35
3½	Bradnop	9 16	2 6		4 46	3 46
5½	Ipstones ¶	9 23	2 13		4 53	3 53
9½	Waterhouses .... arr.	9 35	2 25		5 5	4 5
	dep.	9 50	2 35		5 30	5 5
11½	Sparrowlee	9 56	2 41		5 36	5 11
13½	Beeston Tor	10 4	2 49		5 44	5 19
13¾	Grindon	10 7	2 52		5 47	5 22
14½	Thor's Cave *	1012	2 57		5 52	5 27
15	Redhurst	a	a		a	a
15½	Wetton Mill	1016	3 1		5 56	5 31
16½	Butterton	1023	3 8		6 3	5 38
17	Ecton, for Warslow	1026	3 11		6 6	5 41
18	Hulme End † ....arr.	1030	3 15		6 10	5 45

Miles		Week Days					Suns.
		mrn	mrn	aft		aft	aft
	Hulme End ....dep.	....	8 55	1 25	Wednesdays and Saturdays.	4 5	3 40
1	Ecton, for Warslow	....	8 59	1 29		4 14	3 44
1½	Butterton	....	9 2	1 32		4 17	3 47
2¼	Wetton Mill	....	9 9	1 39		4 24	3 54
3	Redhurst	....	a	a		a	a
3½	Thor's Cave *	....	9 13	1 43		4 28	3 58
4¼	Grindon	....	9 18	1 48		4 33	4 3
4¾	Beeston Tor	....	9 21	1 51		4 36	4 6
6½	Sparrowlee	....	9 29	1 59		4 44	4 14
8½	Waterhouses ¶ .... arr	....	9 35	2 5		4 50	4 20
	dep.	....	9 45	2 35		5 15	4 50
12½	Ipstones	7 10	9 59	2 49		5 29	5 6
14½	Bradnop	7 15	10 5	2 55		5 35	5 15
18	Leek 600, 601, 604 ....arr.	7 33	1015	3 5		5 45	5 25

a Stops when required.
* Station for Wetton.

† Station for Sheen (1½ miles) and Hartington (1½ miles)

¶ "Halts" at Winkhill and at Caldon Low between Ipstones and Waterhouses.

Waterhouses Tickets are available at Caldon Low Halt.

After what has been said it is hardly necessary to point out that the prospects of any light railway improve directly with its length. The longer the run the greater the traffic and the cheaper it can be worked. If a light railway, constructed at a minimum cost per mile, should not make an altogether satisfactory return on capital, the surest remedy is to extend it.

In the case of the Manifold, Calthrop's words fell on deaf ears, and the reason for this is not hard to find: from the outset the Manifold suffered from what in modern parlance would be termed a poor cash-flow position, and simply did not have enough capital to fund any expansion plans on its own, however desirable they might be. When two new transporter wagons were ordered in 1906, for example, only one was paid for outright; the £315 for the other had to be borrowed from the NSR and 4 per cent interest paid on the loan until 1914 when the debt was waived (one transporter arrived in 1907, the second the year after).

Other benefactors made similar concessions. The Treasury suspended interest on its loan in 1909, while the County Council did likewise for five years. Without doubt what kept the railway alive was its milk traffic – hence the order for two new transporter wagons – and especially

The south portal of Swainsley Tunnel, in 1934. The number 21 bridge plate was an LMS addition.
H.C. Casserley

the introduction of a nightly through service of milk wagons to London in 1907, whilst at the same time a Sunday milk run was inaugurated over the line. Other significant sources of goods revenue – apart from coal and beer to Hulme End – so freely talked of while the railway was being planned, never materialised. As for passengers, apart from the welcome crowds on Bank Holidays, the situation is best summed-up by a comment reportedly made by one of the construction navvies on the opening day: 'It's a grand bit of line, but they wunna mak a go on it for it starts from nowheer and finishes up at same place.'

In 1911 the issue of £12,000 debenture stock at 4 per cent was authorised; the following year £8,000 of this was issued and the remainder in 1914; then in 1915 Charles Bill died and, since he had personally guaranteed the Company's bank overdraft, this was paid from his estate. In many ways he, more than anyone else, had been responsible for bringing about the very existence of the line, and for maintaining that existence, and it is sad that the little railway never really lived up to his expectations. By the time of his death the financial arrangement between the L&MVLR Co. and the NSR had been changed once again, this time to a fixed annual payment by the NSR to the Manifold, starting in 1912, of £675 increasing to £750 over a ten-year period. Bill was suceeded as Chairman of the L&MVLR Co. by Hambledon, though he was not replaced as a director. Dealing in the Company's shares was supended in 1913, by which date their value had plummeted to just 6*d* (2.5p)!

In 1918 the Manifold received a welcome boost to its fortunes in the shape of the dairy processing plant, mentioned earlier, built next to the line at Ecton. A siding was laid into the creamery to deal with the increased traffic and the railway's future looked better than it had done for a long time.

Above left: Handbill advertising Saturday excursions from Buxton, including a return trip over the 'Toy Railway'. Although no year is given, the reference to (horse-drawn) 'four-in-hand Char-a-banc' almost certainly dates it to the pre-First World War period.

Above right: After the First World War the internal combustion engine took over from the horse, with excursions from Buxton now being made in far speedier fashion.

Under the LMS

Under the provisions of the Transport Act of 1921, on the landmark date of 1 January 1923 virtually all the railways of Britain – large and small – were 'grouped' into four regional companies, in a move to improve the efficiency of the country's railway system after the neglect it had suffered during the First World War. Although scarcely noticeable at the time, the passing of the NSR and the L&MVLR, and the creation of the new entity of the London Midland & Scottish Railway (LMS), marked the end of an era. The war to end wars had killed the Edwardian age of elegance and leisure, and now the internal combustion engine was about to do the same for the traditional patterns of rural life. Collectively, English light and narrow gauge railways were entering their years of decline. It was a slow, almost imperceptible process, but it was a decline nevertheless, characterised by falling receipts, a lack of expenditure on new stock and a general running-down of all services. The LMS had had to pay the sum of £30,000 for a railway that had a debit balance of £14,000 growing by some £2,000 a year.

It was perhaps fitting that on the Manifold the last new item of rolling-stock, a fifth transporter wagon, was ordered by the NSR, though it actually arrived after the Grouping (see Chapter 5). At the same time all the rolling-stock received new liveries to commemorate the new ownership. Otherwise, the little railway went on much as before with its minimum of stock and staff. Indeed, during the summer it became quite popular with day-trippers who would arrive at one end of the line by motor coach, then journey along it by train before being picked up by the coach at the other terminus. At other times of the year, though, the picture was sadly different – then half a dozen passengers on a train was a fine complement.

On 30 March 1927 Calthrop died, happily before his railway did, although he must have known that the age of the light railway was already coming to an end. Quaint though the Manifold may appear to modern eyes, it should not be forgotten that in 1904 it represented the very latest in narrow gauge railway engineering. Now times were changing, though it is highly probable that Calthrop would have changed with them (always a forward-looking person, it is not often appreciated that in his later years he turned his attention to a new, exciting area of transport: aviation). It is highly likely that had he lived to witness them, he would have approved of the trials undertaken on the Manifold in July 1932 with the chassis of an Armstrong-Whitworth diesel-electric railcar, built for the 2ft 6in gauge Gaekwar of Baroda's State Railway (see Chapter 5 for further details of this and other visitors to the line). No doubt he would also have appreciated the irony of the Manifold, having benefited from one Indian railway at the beginning of its life, in its turn proving of benefit to another at its close.

Happily, the Manifold was captured on film before it died and the story of how the film was taken – and how it has managed to survive – is a fascinating one. In 1932 a film team was in the area and, whilst there, was persuaded by the owner-manager of the Majestic cinema in Leek, a Mr Marriott, to make a film of a run along the line. This the team did, and subsequently presented him with a copy. In 1960 Marriott was persuaded to lend the film to the British Film Insitute to allow a copy to be made for the National Film Archive. If it had not been for prompting by Robert Keys, the film would have been lost for ever, for shortly afterwards the Majestic, and the original film, were destroyed by fire.

An early postcard view of Butterton Station, with Swainsley Hall half-hidden by trees on the left. The northern tunnel portal is out of sight on the right.

Operation

The overall system of working the Manifold was simplicity itself. The railway's two locomotives were both based at Hulme End and were used originally on the 'one engine in steam' principle, which in practice meant that only one locomotive was allowed to be running anywhere on the line at any one time, thus eliminating any possibility of two trains colliding. On the rare occasions both engines did appear, they were always coupled together, for double-heading heavy trains, as 'one engine'. In addition, authorisation for the driver to be out on the line was in the form of a metal tablet, to which was fixed an Annett's key to unlock all the points on the line (other than the automatic pair on the loop at Waterhouses). The coaches were also stabled at Hulme End.

It was soon discovered that whilst ideal from the safety viewpoint, the 'one engine in steam' principle severely hampered the working of the railway: the second engine might be needed for shunting purposes at Hulme End, for example, or to take a second, special train out after a scheduled service had departed. Accordingly, in 1906 the Board of Trade sanctioned the adoption of the 'train staff and ticket' system, whereby a second driver was permitted to venture out onto the line after receiving a written ticket in lieu of the train staff – though not until the preceding train had reached Waterhouses, where it was then required to wait until the arrival of the second train. (The procedure applied in reverse for the journey back to Hulme End.)

The maximum permitted speed of trains on the railway was 30mph, except at ungated level crossings where a 10mph limit was in force.

Manning the trains was very much in keeping with such rural lines: the railway's first driver was Frank Salt who only retired in 1930, to be succeeded for the last four years by the then fireman, Dennis Reynolds. The guard was Arthur Salt, Frank's son, and he stayed with the line from opening to closure – but father and son reportedly never spoke directly to each other, preferring to communicate through the long-term regular fireman, Arthur Dowler! In 1928 the Hulme End shed cleaner, Bob Powner, was transferred to Gloucester, and replaced on the Manifold by Frank Beardmore (who also fired on occasions). The fitter in charge at Hulme End was Leslie Henstock. In every sense, the Manifold was worked for and by its own little community, though men would occasionally be sent in by the NSR or LMS if the line was temporarily short-staffed.

Signalling

There was a total of six signals in use at any one time on the Manifold, arranged in pairs along its length. The first two, controlled from the joint standard/narrow gauge signal box at Waterhouse, were sited one each end of the station run-round loop (before the opening of the terminus proper the temporary station also had a pair of signals consisting of a home and a starting signal mounted on the same post but these were removed when this station closed). The next two were standard NSR ground discs, raised to the driver's eye level and placed one each side of the Ashbourne road crossing. These were worked with the gates, swivelling sideways-on to the train when the way was clear for the driver to proceed. The last two signals were at Hulme End and comprised another home/starting pair on a single post. These were worked from a five-lever ground frame on the platform.

All the signals were supplied and fitted by the NSR, as was the railway's telephone system which comprised a fixed set at each terminus plus a portable handset carried on the train which could be plugged in to the lines at the other stations (except Redhurst Crossing).

Butterton Station in 1934. Little appears to have changed in some three decades, though the bungalow is now somewhat weather-beaten. *H.C. Casserley*

Immediately beyond Butterton Station was the district known as Ecton Lea. This G. Hill & Sons of Leek postcard shows Naylor's Temperance Hotel centre shot; the field below to the right was a sometime bowling green. In the distance a two-coach train approaches, a little to the left of the huts formerly used to house the railway's construction workers (and the site of the smallpox outbreak).

As mentioned above, the solitary signal box at Waterhouses had a dual role in that it controlled standard gauge operations at the station as well. It is believed to have been constructed by the NSR to a design supplied by the well-known Worcester signal equipment firm of McKenzie & Holland Ltd; it certainly housed an M&H 10-lever frame of which seven levers were allocated to the standard gauge layout and two to the narrow gauge, with one left spare.

Passenger services

The Manifold's first scheduled timetable and fares list, as advertised for the railway's opening, was as follows:

				A	B	A	3rd class fares from Hulme End	
							Single	Return
Hulme End	dep.	9.05	11.35	2.30	5.10	7.40		
Ecton	'	9.10	11.40	2.35	5.16	7.45	1d	2d
Butterton	'	9.13	11.43	2.38	5.20	7.48	2d	3d
Wetton Mill	'	9.19	11.49	2.44	5.27	7.54	3d	5d
Thor's Cave	'	9.24	11.54	2.49	5.32	7.59	4d	7d
Grindon	'	9.29	11.59	2.54	5.38	8.04	5d	8d
Beeston Tor	'	9.32	12.02	2.57	5.41	8.07	5d	8d
Sparrowlee	'	9.42	12.12	3.07	5.52	8.17	7d	1s
Waterhouses	arr.	9.50	12.20	3.15	6.00	8.25	9d	1s 3d

				A	B	A	3rd class fares from Waterhouses	
							Single	Return
Waterhouses	dep.	10.05	12.30	3.30	6.15	8.40		
Sparrowlee	'	10.13	12.38	3.38	6.23	8.48	2d	3d
Beeston Tor	'	10.23	12.48	3.48	6.34	8.58	4d	7d
Grindon	'	10.26	12.51	3.51	6.37	9.01	4d	7d
Thor's Cave	'	10.31	12.56	3.56	6.43	9.06	5d	8d
Wetton Mill	'	10.36	1.01	4.01	6.48	9.11	6d	10d
Butterton	'	10.42	1.07	4.07	6.55	9.17	7d	1s
Ecton	'	10.45	1.10	4.10	6.59	9.20	8d	1s 1d
Hulme End	arr.	10.50	1.15	4.15	7.05	9.25	9d	1s 3d

A – Thursday and Saturdays only
B – Thursday and Saturdays excepted

Market tickets issued on Wednesdays and Saturdays cost 1s 6d (7.5p) return from Hulme End and 1s 3d (6p) from all other stations. Ticket offices were sited at each terminus whilst passengers from intermediate stops were catered for by the guard, who carried a supply of tickets for this purpose. On Mondays, Thursdays and Saturdays cheap excursion tickets could be bought at Stoke to any station on the line for 3s (15p); by 1934 this had risen to 3s 9d (19p) for specified trains on Wednesday, Thursday, Saturday and Sunday, with a ticket for 5s 6d (27.5p) also available from Crewe. Surviving examples of any kind are rare.

Although the printed caption implies this is Ecton Station, it is fact Thor's Cave, this being the less common (postcard) view northwards, away from the cave.

Ecton, Manifold Valley.

The genuine Ecton Station. The view is again to the north, from the loop.

River and Railway,
Manifold Valley.

Beyond Ecton, anyone looking out of a Hulme End-bound train would have noticed the head of the valley slowly starting to open out, as on this W. Shaw of Burslem coloured postcard. The railway now gradually diverges from the river for the last half mile or so of its journey.

This was the pattern for the Manifold's services for most of its life, with Sunday services added in 1905, dropped in 1906, then reinstated. Some summers saw six or seven trains a day, whilst during the winter months the scheduled service was cut to just three. There were, however, times – for example at Bank Holidays – when the railway's four coaches could not cope with the crowds on offer and on these occasions all the available open goods wagons would be equipped with temporary seats and coupled up. With both locomotives steaming majestically at the head of the train, all the line's rolling-stock, with the sole exception of the covered van, could well be on the move together in a continuous shuttle service! From June 1906, passengers on the Manifold train could post letters in a special Travelling Letter Box which was conveyed, over the standard gauge branch, every night to Leek station for the mail to be reposted there; no charge was made for using this service.

Goods services

Strictly speaking, goods traffic was not separable from the passenger since mixed working was the norm, with goods wagons being picked up and dropped off by trains en route as the need arose (on some occasions, wagons would even be loaded or unloaded whilst passengers patiently waited!). Such a method of operation was necessitated by the line's 'one engine in steam' principle of working, but no great inconvenience was caused since any prolonged shunting activities were normally confined to Waterhouses, Ecton and Hulme End. Besides, an unhurried railway was in keeping with both its time and its valley.

by that section for transhipment of merchandise in respect of Railway (No. 4) shall in the case of merchandise of one ton and upwards in weight be one penny halfpenny for each ton or fraction of a ton over a complete number of tons and in the case of merchandise under one ton in weight be determined in case of difference in manner provided by that section.

43. For the conveyance upon Railway (No. 4) of small parcels not exceeding five hundred pounds in weight by passenger train the Company may demand and take any charges not exceeding the following (that is to say) :— *(Charges for small parcels upon Railway (No. 4).)*

  For any parcel not exceeding seven pounds in weight three pence ;

  For any parcel exceeding seven pounds but not exceeding fourteen pounds in weight five pence ;

  For any parcel exceeding fourteen pounds but not exceeding twenty-eight pounds in weight seven pence ;

  For any parcel exceeding twenty-eight pounds but not exceeding fifty-six pounds in weight nine pence ;

  And for any parcel exceeding fifty-six pounds but not exceeding five hundred pounds in weight the Company may demand any sum they think fit :

Provided that articles sent in large aggregate quantities although made up in separate parcels such as bags of sugar coffee meal and the like shall not be deemed small parcels but that term shall apply only to single parcels in separate packages.

44. The maximum rate of charges to be made by the Company for the conveyance of passengers upon Railway (No. 4) including every expense incidental to such conveyance shall not exceed the following (that is to say) :— *(Maximum rates for passengers upon Railway (No. 4).)*

  For every passenger conveyed in a first-class carriage three pence per mile :

  For every passenger conveyed in a second-class carriage two pence per mile :

  For every passenger conveyed in a third-class carriage one penny per mile :

  For every passenger conveyed on the said railway for a less distance than three miles the Company may charge as for three miles and every fraction of a mile beyond three miles or any greater number of miles shall be deemed a mile.

45. Every passenger travelling upon Railway (No. 4) may take with him his ordinary luggage not exceeding one hundred pounds in weight for first-class passengers sixty pounds in weight for second-class passengers and forty pounds in weight for third-class passengers without any charge being made for the carriage thereof. *(Passengers luggage upon Railway (No. 4))*

46. The restrictions as to the charges to be made for passengers shall not extend to any special train run upon Railway (No. 4) in respect of which the Company may make such charges as they think fit but shall apply only to the ordinary and express trains appointed from time to time by the Company for the conveyance of passengers and goods upon the said railway. *(Foregoing charges not to apply to special trains.)*

The Manifold's permitted charges for (from the top) general merchandise, parcels, and passengers and their luggage as laid down in the 1898 LRO.

Waterhouses was the main focus for the railway's dairy traffic and in the early days was the scene of frenzied bursts of activity whenever a train arrived. Porters would appear, empty churns would be lined up on the platform, full ones trundled off the wagons on barrows and the empties loaded on for their journey back to their farms. The train gone, all would be quiet again with only a disproportionate number of barrows resting on the platform to arouse curiosity in an observant mind. The whole scene would then be repeated at length with the standard gauge train. Over much of rural England such goings-on were commonplace, though are now long-vanished, and the daily milk train from Waterhouses direct to London had its innumerable counterparts in other farming regions. Much of the traffic was later carried by the line's transporters, rather than by its open wagons, and, when the glass-lined bulk tanker wagon displaced at least part of the role of the humble 17-gallon churn, Calthrop's invention really came into its own, carrying the tankers all the way from Ecton creamery to United Dairies' Finsbury Park facility.

The transporters

Possibly the most commented-upon aspect of the Manifold's operation, these wagons were of simple design, easy to use and eminently practical — in short, a typical example of Calthrop's ideas in action. He began working on their invention in the late 1890s and their adoption was approved by the Manifold directors in 1902; their success in England led to their later use on the Barsi Light Railway — though it is worth recording that Calthrop regarded their use in India as not particularly justified, noting in his 1897 paper that:

The advantages of avoiding transshipment in England are considerably greater than in India, where the low cost of labour makes it generally preferable to transship goods rather than incur the haulage of additional dead weight.

A major obstacle to be overcome in the efficient operation of a narrow gauge railway is that posed by the transshipment of goods. Paradoxically, the more successful a narrow gauge line is in terms of volume of freight carried, the greater the problem. One tried and tested solution at the time of the Manifold's construction was to carry narrow gauge wagons, loads and all, on broader gauge ones. Thus, in North Wales, loaded narrow gauge slate wagons were transported by 'main line' from quarry to port, each load travelling untouched from source to quayside without a direct narrow gauge link between the two. This system was used notably by the LNWR (with 4ft 8½in gauge transporter wagons) and the Padarn Railway (4ft). Calthrop's brilliant invention literally turned this operation upside-down: standard gauge wagons would be transported on narrow gauge ones, which meant that once loaded at source, goods could be moved untouched to anywhere on the country's rail network. The only drawback was that the narrow gauge line had to be built to a standard loading gauge – or larger – in order to accommodate the loaded transporters, though this still proved considerably cheaper than laying a standard gauge line.

The Manifold was so planned by Calthrop and, as has been noted earlier, most of the stations were equipped with a short standard gauge section where wagons could be left awaiting their freight. The narrow gauge tracks in the goods yard at Waterhouses led of course straight onto standard gauge ones, where two sidings were normally used for the loading of standard gauge wagons on to transporters, with one longer one allocated for the reverse operation. Capstans were available to move the heaviest of wagons, though two men could generally man-handle most of them. Remarkably, the normal time elapsing between positioning the transporter at the buffers and securing a wagon on it was just eighty-five seconds. Technical and other details of these vehicles can be found in Chapter 5.

Calthrop's ingenious design was a great success and from the very outset attracted much attention and favourable comment in the technical press. Typical was that made by the *Railway Magazine* of September 1904: 'the general introduction of such vehicles should have a considerable effect on the extension of narrow gauge lines, by removing the strongest objection to their use as feeders to railways of the standard gauge'. For the other narrow gauge railways of Britain though, hampered by their existing restricted loading gauges, the 'general introduction of such vehicles' was, alas, impossible. One intriguing 'might have been' deserves mention. In August 1897 Calthrop gave evidence to the public enquiry into an application for a LRO which resulted, six years later, in the opening of the 2ft 6in gauge Welshpool & Llanfair Light Railway in mid-Wales (consequently just pipping the Manifold to the post.) At the enquiry – also attended by Col Boughey in his role as one of the Light Railway Commissioners – Calthrop advocated the use of transporter wagons to avoid trans-shipment problems at Welshpool where the line was to connect with the national standard gauge network. So certain was he that this would come to pass that he included, in his 1897 paper, the confident assertion that transporters…

…will be employed on the Welshpool-Llanfair 2ft 6in. gauge Light Railway, recently sanctioned by the Light Railway Commissioners. In this case they will be used for the transportation of fully loaded 4ft 8½in gauge railway wagons over the narrow gauge line.

As things transpired, this was not to be the case, though the Cambrian Railways – which worked the Welsh line much as the NSR worked the Manifold – did go so far as to draw up plans for such a vehicle.

Finally, to end this chapter on the Manifold at work, two early postcard views of Hulme End: from the end of the platform...

... and from the goods sidings. Here *J.B. Earle* waits to depart with a laden two-coach train.
Courtesy Peter Treloar

Accidents

Reports of accidents – of any sort – on the Manifold are rare. The only incident of any seriousness reportedly took place at Ecton, date unknown. Milk had been loaded one morning onto a six-wheel LMS van in the siding, and this vehicle was being man-handled onto a transporter wagon when – with two axles only on the transporter – the engine driver started the train. The undamaged churns rescued from the resulting derailment had to be loaded into other (presumably narrow gauge) wagons before they could continue their journey.

The only accident involving the coaches occurred during the summer of 1904 – but not on the Manifold! It appears that the railway's second pair of new coaches were damaged when their transporting wagons were shunted at Macclesfield whilst on their way from Preston to Waterhouses, necessitating carriage No.3 being mended at Hulme End and No.4 returning to the makers for repairs.

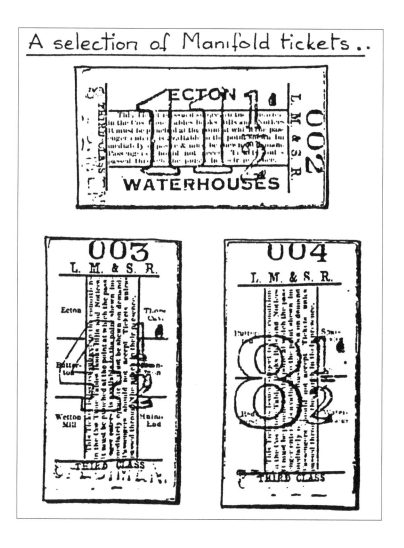

four
Death

The End of an Age

For many of Britain's light and narrow gauge railways the 1930s was the end of an age. Of those lines that entered the years of the Second World War, few emerged unscathed. It was the decade when the motor bus truly took over as many people's choice of public transport, especially in rural areas. Among narrow gauge lines the Festiniog, the Welshpool & Llanfair, the Corris, the Campbeltown & Machrihanish, the Ashover, the Glyn Valley, the Lynton & Barnstaple, the Rye & Camber and the Welsh Highland all lost their passenger services during those ten years and, for some, their goods traffic as well. For all those lines the writing, in the form of closure announcements, was literally on the wall. For the Manifold the prospect was equally grim. In 1932 the Ecton creamery closed and the whole of the valley's milk traffic was reorganised, based on road collection and transport to a new dairy at Rowsley, and the Manifold's part in this traffic ceased. (The principal reason advanced by the dairy company for the closure of the creamery – and thus indirectly the railway – was its refusal, on the grounds of cost, to install a new effluent treatment plant to stop river pollution.) It was clear that sooner, rather than later, the railway would be killed off as yet another victim of Britain's continually changing pattern of transport use.

Before we come to the sad, final moments, a nostalgic reminder of what the Manifold was really like to know and love brings out so much of the unique atmosphere of these small, hidden-away, narrow gauge lines. The following passage describes a journey over the line made in the summer of 1933 – its last summer of operation – and, despite some trifling errors of detail, surely captures the special atmosphere of the Manifold better than any photograph. It is from *The Peak: Some People and Places*, by Bernard Casson and Jean Thorburn, published in 1933 by J.W. Northend Ltd of Sheffield. (One printing error has been corrected.)

I have found a railway. It is about twenty miles long, and has ten stations. It took me one and quarter hours to reach it by car from Sheffield, fifty minutes to go the full length of the line, half an hour's rest, and fifty minutes back. There was a day of adventure for you!

I found Hulme End Station as we turned a corner of the road two miles from the village of Hartington. The railway rejoices in the name of The Leek and Manifold Valley Light Railway. This is on a brass plate on the engine, which, when I arrived, was puffing softly to let the driver know that all was well and ready for the start.

The engine driver, meanwhile, was sitting on the kerbstone, which marks the difference between the platform and the railroad, reading his morning paper.

He was a cheery soul, with very blue eyes and white teeth, and he enjoys his railway. I am quite sure of that. It has existed since 1904, and he has spent nine years as driver, so he knows a good deal about it. At one time, he told me, the railway was the "Milky Way" of the district. Hundreds of gallons of milk were carried from its little stations to the main line. Now there is no great distribution of milk, but Manchester "hikers" love the railway, and so do the holiday parties, who leave their charabancs at Hulme End and do the railway trip while the cars proceed by a longer road to Waterhouse [sic], and there pick them up.

Death: *E.R. Calthrop* was brought out of storage in February 1937 to haul the demolition train. This Railway Photographs of Liverpool postcard shows its rather sorry-looking appearance at the time.

About 500 holiday makers, mostly from the Potteries, travel on this line on August Bank Holiday. There are three trains a day, one in the morning, the next at 1 p.m., and the third at 4 p.m. I booked for the lunch-time train, and had three companions, a lady, a gentleman and a little boy.

There was an air of great peace over the station until about 12.50, when everyone seemed to get busy at once. The stationmaster and a porter suddenly remembered about a load of coal and a couple of carriages which should be elsewhere, so the engine driver got busy and his mate began shunting these obstacles.

Now this railway is a small gauge affair, but the coal wagons are of the ordinary size, so they have to be brought along on "transports", which are iron platforms fitting the small gauge lines to take the wagons. There is one siding with ordinary gauge, and the wagons had to be landed there while the extra carriages had to be put in the shed, in case they were blistered by the sun. All this took twenty minutes and the guard didn't like it. He wanted to run to time. At 1.20 we were off down the valley of the lost rivers. The coach was divided into first and third class. There was a slight difference in the upholstery, and as the engine ran backwards on this journey, the first class got more smoke, which didn't really matter, as we were all third class passengers.

My companion, the photographer, deserted me for the front of the train, where he stood on a little platform to get some of the views. I watched the beauties of the Manifold Valley, softly rounded hills, with wooded slopes, a river with crystal clear water, a profusion of wild flowers. We passed a field where a snow-white tent shone in the sun, and we rolled along in the heart of the valley.

The engine driver ignored the stations on the way out; we passed Ecton (for Warslow) almost before I noticed it. Several of the stations were not marked by buildings, merely by name signs, and others are important enough to have sheds for shelter. Butterton was next, and then a tunnel. Then Wetton Mill, where children with bouquets of forget-me-nots waved to us from a nearby field.

Somewhere near here I noticed that we no longer saw the river, only a dry watercourse, which we crossed and re-crossed for the rest of the way. Dry, dusty stones looked hot in the sun, plantations spread their shade over

PUBLIC NOTICE

Notice is hereby given that the

Manifold Valley Light Railway Section

of the Company's Line

WATERHOUSES to HULME END

will be CLOSED for the conveyance
of ALL classes of traffic on and from
MONDAY, MARCH 12th, 1934

BY ORDER.

District Goods and
    Passenger Manager's Office,
      Stoke-on-Trent,
March 1st, 1934.

The Company have excellent facilities for dealing
with PASSENGERS, GOODS and MINERALS
Traffic at the following Stations, covering the
WATERHOUSES to HULME END area:-

ALSOP-EN-LE-DALE	TISSINGTON
HARTINGTON	WATERHOUSES
IPSTONES	WINKHILL
THORPE CLOUD	

The Manifold's official notice of closure, issued
on 1 March 1934. There was to be no reprieve.

E.R. Calthrop with the long transporter, working as the demolition train near Ecton. No.1's ignominious
fate was to be cut up at Waterhouses that October. *Courtesy Peter Treloar*

the dry river, and here and there tufts of grass and dried moss were on the rounded stones, while the well-built stone bridges looked quite out of place and useless.

We came to Red Hurst Crossing. In front I saw hills grow higher and lose their roundness. A sharp peak towered above us and we reached Thor's Cave, which was high up on the left. Then we came to Grindon, and then to Beeston Tor, then to Sparrowlee, and we were running out of the valley to see a wider sweep of country.

We had to cross a main road and that took time, as the fireman got down and closed the gates against the traffic. After he had climbed back into the engine we moved on a little, and the guard opened the gates and climbed back into the carriage. We moved on again, and in a minute or two drew up at Waterhouse, where the railway finds its big brother, the Leek Railway. Here, too, we saw the river again.

I asked the guard one or two questions about the stream, but he was not talkative and I was little the wiser. But on our return to the train I met those cheery fellows who drive the engine, and they described the days when the watercourses were full. They told me that had I walked a short distance from the village, I should have seen the water of the Hamps suddenly disappear underground. Where it comes out no one knows. The Manifold does not present so great a mystery. It disappears near Wetton and comes out at Ilam, but the Hamps, after the pretty village of Waterhouse, disappears for good.

As we came back through the valley I pondered over this story. It is a fairy tale in real life – the valley of the lost river, with its lovely woods and rich fields, its wild roses and forget-me-nots, and meadow sweet. Its loveliness seems to smile at the mere humans who cannot know the secret of its river. The flowers and the trees and the birds could tell of the watercourse, for in the quietness when no fussy little train with its freight of noisy human beings is about, they may hear the trickle of water underground.

I was awakened out of this dreamland by the train drawing up with a jerk. No one got off, no one got on, but the guard, the engine driver and the fireman exchanged greetings with a pretty girl who was making hay in the field beside the railway. I do not wonder that they wanted to talk to her, she looked so cheery and brown and happy. Her rounded arms were a lovely brown against the lighter colour of her dress, and her wavy hair was unshaded by hat and unspoilt by "perm". We went on again but pulled up at Wetton, where the children with the forget-me-nots climbed aboard; they waved to the engine driver as he opened his little window and took coals from the tiny tender. Two men got on board, and as we had seven passengers instead of five, we were quite a company.

The guard came and took our tickets in silent sternness. How stupid we were to be excited or even interested in the valley he went through several times a day! The engine driver bade us a cherry "good-bye" as we stepped out of the train, and hoped that we had enjoyed the run. The children waved their flowers at him and ran off laughing.

Rumour has it that this line is to be closed, but no one could tell us if this really was the case. The railway will go on; the engine puff its way with its load of carriages and passengers, sometimes half a dozen, sometimes a hundred. But the Manifold Valley is lovely and mysterious, with its unknown railway and its lost rivers.

As we got into the car we took a look back at the green hills, with their fine trees, at the outline against the sky, and we turned to go towards the real world, for this ended our adventures on a day when we found a railway and lost two rivers.

Closure

On 21 February 1934 the Traffic Committee of the LMS took the decision to close the Manifold. It was a straightforward commercial decision, based on the calculation that closure (to all traffic) would result in an immediate saving of £773 a year of working expenses over revenue, even without taking the extra burden of maintenance costs into consideration. Perhaps

The station bungalow at Thor's Cave, captured on a William J.B. Blake of Longton postcard shortly after the railway track bed had been turned into a footpath – apart from which, nothing has changed from pre-closure views of the station.

even more important though was the fact that an estimated £13,840 needed to be spent on renewing the permanent way, Calthrop's track apparently having finally reached the end of its life. It was not a snap decision either, for the LMS had taken pains to ensure that it was legally entitled to close the railway by obtaining, in its London Midland & Scottish Railway Act of 1933, the necessary statutory powers enabling it to do so.

No time was seemingly wasted on second thoughts – such as how expenses might perhaps be reduced or revenue increased – for just a week later, on 1 March, the LMS issued a notice to the effect that the Manifold would be closed to all classes of traffic on and from Monday 12 March 1934. There being no Sunday service, this meant that the last scheduled train was the Saturday Hulme End to Waterhouses and back on 10 March. Having brought the contents of Hulme End station building to Waterhouses, the train, consisting of a locomotive and one carriage plus a handful of goods wagons, left Waterhouses some thirty to forty minutes late (accounts vary slightly) with a grand total of seven passengers aboard, one of whom alighted at Grindon, the only intermediate stop made (this is believed to have been seventy-eight-year-old William Wood, owner of the nearby Beeston Tor Farm, Company shareholder and refreshment room proprietor, who had travelled on the railway's very first train as well).

By all accounts it must have been a visually impressive trip with snow in the air, mist clinging to the valley sides and three inches of snow on the ground. It must also have been rather a chilly one considering the lack of under-seat heating in the carriage! In the words of D.M. Smith, writing in the *Railway Magazine* in May 1934:

At Hulme End, the terminus, reality returned, for it seemed as if we had passed through a valley of dreams. There was considerable activity here – a place which consists of several cottages and a Light Railway Hotel, now, alas, an anachronism – as after all, even on a light railway the last day of service must have a certain importance.

And that was that. Fittingly, its demise was in every sense as leisurely an affair as its construction and life had been. *J.B. Earle* was moved to Crewe works and put into store (for what envisaged eventuality – sale to the Great Western Railway for use on its Welshpool & Llanfair Light Railway perhaps?) while the rest of the stock was collected by *E.R. Calthrop* and gathered together at Waterhouses, the locomotive protected by a tarpaulin. The following year one of the transporters was sold to the narrow gauge Ashover Light Railway in Derbyshire. Some local voices were raised in protest at the closure, but not many, for the idea had been mooted of somehow turning the track bed into a roadway so that some benefit at least could be gained from the railway's abandonment. The LMS considered the suggestion, weighed up any other possibilities, then put paid to any lingering hopes of a Manifold revival by running its last passenger train over the Leek to Waterhouses branch on Saturday, 28 September 1935 (with official closure from the following Monday). In 1936, having decided that it was time it did something else, the LMS announced its intention of dismantling the narrow gauge line, whereupon local pressure was put on the County Council to buy the track bed and convert it into a road or footpath. The rails, and some of the vehicles, were sold in situ to a Mr Twigg of Matlock and cut up on site or otherwise disposed of whilst George Cohen, Sons & Co. Ltd, of Stanningley in Leeds, were awarded the demolition contract. Using *E.R. Calthrop* and the goods stock, Cohens began work in February 1937 on lifting the track (and scrapped *J.B. Earle* at their yard).

For a description of just how quickly the remains of the Manifold railway began to decay after closure, I can do no better than to quote from the September 1936 journal of G.V. Wingfield-Digby, a copy of which was kindly sent me by its author following the appearance of the first edition of this history. In it he paints, in words, an evocative portrait of the railway's decrepitude as he found it during his explorations that month. The following two passages make for especially poignant reading:

Wednesday 9 September. Before the Halt of Butterton (miles from the village it served) there was a tunnel – the only bore on the line. What a dismal place, with the water trickling and streaming down the walls, with a tiny glare of daylight peeping in at either end. It seemed to become darker as one advanced further into it, and our voices echoed weirdly against the slimy walls. It was sad to think that it is now two years since the last little train thundered through it, and that, never more, will it be of any further use, but only (even as ourselves) await the day that it will tumble in and decay to its extermination. Just beyond was yet another hollow iron bridge, extremely rusty, and with the river gurgling and chattering far below.

Friday 11 September. During the fore-noon I examined the deserted station of Hulme End – the little terminus of the narrow-gauge railway that 'ran from No-where to No-where', as it was aptly described.

It was a depressing sight – overgrown, rusty and forlorn. The name-board lay on its face across the track in a melancholy fashion; and, when I tried to raise it, I found it rotting away. Besides the usual offices and waiting-rooms (locked, but looking dismal enough through the broken windows) there are various sheds for engines and rolling-stock (all empty, but in good condition); a decayed coal-tip, and several overgrown sidings. It was indeed the 'dead-end' of a very sorry wreck of a most attractive railway...

The Footpath – and after

That sorry picture, thankfully, was about to change. Even as the railway was being dismantled, the LMS donated the track bed to Staffordshire County Council who arranged to turn it into the requested footpath at a cost of £6,000, using Cohens to do the work of shifting the stone needed for metalling the path from the Caldon Low quarries. The finished footpath was opened by Sir Josiah Stamp, President of the LMS, in a simple ceremony at 3.30 p.m. on Friday 23 July 1937. As can be inferred from the low cost of its construction, the relatively simple conversion task involved little more than the levelling and surfacing of the former railway track bed, and the repair of some of the bridges; buildings and other structures along the path were left intact. The whole of the old line was so converted, with the sole exception of the short stretch from Waterhouses station down to the Ashbourne Road level crossing; this portion was abandoned with access to the path made from the highway.

The conversion of the track bed into a footpath, however, had by no means been a foregone conclusion. Several people living in the area would rather have seen it turned into a road and an Area Committee, with some local authorities' support, was formed to campaign for such a

Wetton Mill on another Blake postcard, showing the Manifold Valley stretching away as far as Thor's Cave (top right), shortly after the new footpath had been laid. The station bungalow still stands, just visible on the extreme right. The senders wrote, on 14 November 1937, that, 'The weather has been lovely although cold, even the river being frozen over.'

course of action. In the event its lobbying of the County Council was unsuccessful, though this did not prevent it from issuing an impassioned, but belated and ill-argued, 'Statement' leaflet, setting out its case, on the day of the footpath's official opening. In essence, the pro-road case was presented as follows:

A MOTOR ROAD on the track of the railway would provide easy access from the district to the main roads and bus routes which exist at Hulme End and Waterhouses. Travellers from the south would find the road a gateway to the villages bordering on the valley, and to good roads leading to Buxton, Bakewell, Matlock and other parts of north-west Derbyshire and beyond…

Now that the light railway has been ABANDONED by the LMS Company, it is claimed that the local people who established the railway by their labours and sacrifices have a moral right to first consideration in the disposal of the residue of their own creation. £50,000 was expended on providing this railway track for the definite purpose of carrying passengers and goods for the benefit of the district. The value still remains if the track is used for its proper purpose as a roadway…

The Area Committee contend that this 'pseudo-footpath' is of no benefit to the county ratepayers, county and other local government officials, doctors, and veterinary surgeons, the real ramblers, the lover of the countryside, or any section…

Judging by the outcome, the road lobby was apparently not yet the force it was to become just a few decades later.

Inevitably, time did not stand still with respect to the remainder of the local rail network. Goods services between Leek and Waterhouses were terminated by the LMS from Monday 1 March 1943 with the closure of that portion of the branch between the village and Caldon Junction (where the branch from the quarries joined the line). Much of the station site at Waterhouses was then cleared, though this took well over a decade to accomplish for the *Railway Magazine* reported in September 1953 that the platform, stop blocks and a length of track survived, as did the level crossing gates on the Ashbourne road. Happily, stone traffic from the Caldon Low quarries provided a very good reason for keeping open − if intermittently − that last section of the original grand light railway plan of the 1890s (one major contract supplied from here was for the Thames Barrage construction work in the late 1970s).

Later work at Waterhouses, during the 1960s, saw the removal of the level crossing gates and much of the former narrow gauge station site scooped away to accommodate a widened Ashbourne road (the A523); soon the only structure left standing was the old goods shed.

At Hulme End, the passage of time proved not quite so harsh as the whole station site became littered with concrete posts, heaps of gravel and the like which manifested its occupation by the County Council's Highways Department. Although the carriage shed was demolished and two smaller garages erected in its stead, left standing were, remarkably, the old wooden station building and the corrugated iron engine shed.

As for the intermediate stations, their tangible remains − wooden buildings, name boards, benches and all − were left to slowly rot away. Some relics survived the years of the Second World War but all were probably gone by 1953 when the track bed footpath between Redhurst Crossing and Butterton (including the stretch through Swainsley Tunnel) was re-laid as a road for motor vehicles. It is tempting to wonder just what Calthrop would have thought of such a turn of events. This was the last major change seen in the valley to date, though in 1959 proposals were made to extend the track bed roadway south from Redhurst as far as Grindon, where it would have joined the Grindon-Wetton road just south of the station by Weags Bridge. Thankfully, public protests by lovers of the valley − including a mass demonstration at Wetton Mill − put paid to the idea.

five
Rolling-stock

The general and operational history of the Manifold's stock has been covered earlier; what now follows is a more detailed account of its design and construction. Such a close look is certainly worthy of its subject for, although few in number, the various items of rolling-stock were far from small in size and far from short in innovative design features. All the stock was built to Calthrop's own specifications, based on his experiments and experience on the Barsi Light Railway; indeed, the influence of the one line upon the other was at once visually obvious. In the words of the *Locomotive Magazine* of 15 July 1904:

In designing the rolling stock Mr. Calthrop followed his system of adopting a uniform axle weight of 5 tons throughout, thereby reducing the weight of and wear on the permanent way to a minimum, and enabling the stock to be constructed with the maximum carrying capacity combined with the minimum of tare weight.

Plates proclaiming the fact that they had been constructed to Calthrop's own designs were carried on the locomotives' bunkers, on the ends of the transporters, and on the sides of wagons and coaches; the latter vehicles also had the same wording emblazoned above the internal doorways dividing their seating areas.

The Locomotives

Two identical 2-6-4 side tank locomotives – believed to be the first tank engines of this wheel arrangement to run in Great Britain – were built for the Manifold in 1904 by Kitson & Co., builders of the Calthrop-designed Barsi engines, and were essentially no more than shortened adaptations, with slightly smaller cylinders, of the Indian line's original 0-8-4 side tanks. (This statement is by no means a criticism of the builders but a commentary on the excellence of Calthrop's original design. Indeed, the design continued to evolve with Kitson's subsequently building 4-8-4s to a Calthrop design, for the Barsi railway, based on operational experience with the Manifold engines!) Even in their smaller details, the Manifold engines betrayed their parentage with their spacious double-roofed cabs (for protection against the sun), a huge headlamp mounted above the smokebox and boltholes in the buffer beams for affixing cowcatchers, though these latter attachments were never fitted on the Manifold and the wooden plugs used to fill the holes soon worked themselves out. A plate on the cab back provided a mounting for the headlamp when running bunker-first although it seems a virtual certainty that the acetylene-carbide lamps were never moved from their imposing station in front of the chimney (and probably never lit either).

In basic terms, the design was a 2-6-4 side tank with outside frames, Walschaert's valve gear and horizontally-mounted outside cylinders driving, via shielded crossheads, onto the rear coupled wheels. An interesting feature of the wheels themselves was that balance weights were not fixed to them in the conventional fashion but were instead carried on brackets attached to the ends of the axles; a second feature was:

Rolling-stock: Locomotive No.1 *E.R.Calthrop* on shed at Hulme End, by the travelling hoist used for minor repair jobs.

No.2 *J.B.Earle* receiving attention in the works at Crewe in LMS days. Note the shorter pop valve and lack of a builder's plate on the bunker.

River Manifold, near Thor's Cave, North Stafford Railway

From Beeston Tor to Redhurst Crossing the railway followed the River Manifold closely along its west bank and it was on this stretch, just north of Grindon Station, that what probably became the single most reproduced image of the Manifold was captured. This original example has the locomotive and coaches in their original liveries; later issues after the demise of the NSR have them retouched in LMS colours.

...an ingenious device, which relieves the leading driving wheel flanges from the excessive strain usually caused in turning the weight of the engine when either leaving or entering a curve. This strain is transformed from the flanges of the leading driving wheels to those of the leading bogie; this is done gradually as the springs [on this two-wheel radial truck] are compressed, and that shock is avoided which takes place if the engine has to be turned by the flanges of wheels which are unable to move in a lateral direction.
(The *Tramway and Railway World*, 14 July 1904)

Rather than having separate buffers and couplers, the locomotives – like the rest of the stock – sported a single Jones-Calthrop Patent Flexible Buffer-Coupling in the centre of each buffer beam. This was basically the Jones Patent Flexible Buffer as used on the Indian metre gauge railways, with rocking dishes added by Calthrop to permit it to move laterally through thirty-six degrees so as to permit coupling of vehicles on tight curves and to reduce flange wear. Each coupling had a buffing plate, some 15in wide and 9in high, which was engaged by a hook on the coupling of the abutting vehicle and the whole tightened by large screws to prevent any slack between them.

Other features of the engines were two injectors and a pump, a left-hand driving position and vacuum braking equipment. They were designed to be able to haul a load of 100 tons at a speed of 8mph.

As delivered, the locomotives were numbered and named 1 *E.R. Calthrop* (works number 4258) and 2 *J.B. Earle* (works number 4257); neither names nor stock numbers were changed during their lives. Some minor alterations were made to them however, beginning with the substitution of large and small whistles for the engines' original large and small hooters (mounted on the front of the cab) before the line opened, presumably as the sounds of the former were found to carry further – especially useful on the approach to the level crossing at Waterhouses. A second small drawback was that the motion was quickly discovered to be prone to overheating and so their covers were permanently removed. Further changes made just before the First World War were the replacement of each locomotive's two Ramsbottom safety valves by a single Ross pop type, and the raising of the bunker behind the cab with sheeting to increase coal capacity (which necessitated the removal of the rear lamp bracket). The last alteration made was the fitting of pipes to water the rails in front of the engine in a successful attempt to cut down the squeaking made by the rolling-stock on the curves; the disadvantage though was that in the autumn months it tended to produce greasy rails and subsequent slipping of the locomotives. All these modifications were made to both engines.

The basic locomotive livery was originally a light, milk chocolate brown with white double lining, with black for the chimney, smokebox and frames. The top of the chimney was burnished brass or copper (as were other smaller attachments of these metals, such as the whistles and pipework), and the motion, handrails, smokebox door and hinges all burnished steel. The buffer beams were vermilion, edged with black and lined in white. The main brown colour was changed at Stoke at the time of the pre-1919 alterations to standard NSR madder-lake with a cream single line, while the headlamps, originally brown, soon shone brightly as the paint was rubbed off the brass; the madder-lake was also used to cover the burnished steel of the handrails and smokebox door. In LMS days the livery was altered – possibly on one engine only – to crimson-lake, edged with black and straw-yellow, with the railway company's insignia on the bunker, though this too was later changed to unlined, unadorned black in the late 1920s (for both locos). The combined number, name and works plates, and the 'Calthrop-designed' plates, carried by each engine retained a red background to their brass letters throughout the railway's life (though possibly they were painted black for a brief period under the LMS).

No.2's combined name/number/works plate. *H.C. Casserley*

As is only to be expected, the histories of the two engines occasionally diverge. When delivered, both faced the same way on the line, bunker towards Hulme End. After one bout of attention at Crewe – believed to have been c.1930 – E.R. Calthrop was returned and re-railed in the reverse fashion. The theory was then advanced that, with a low level of water in the boiler, the steep ascent into Waterhouses might result in the firebox crown burning out when the engine came in bunker-first. In the event, such fears proved groundless and E.R. Calthrop was not turned 'right way round' until a further visit to Crewe, in 1934, just weeks before the line closed. Other, more minor differences that developed over the years included the loss of the builder's plates from the bunker of J.B. Earle and their replacement by circular LMS crests (this engine also had slightly shorter pop valves and a slightly taller, narrower steam dome than its sister) and the fitting of a handle on one side of the smokebox door of E.R. Calthrop, presumably to make it easier to open.

J.B. Earle was officially withdrawn on 23 February 1935, having been stored at Crewe since the previous year, and in May 1937 she was sold to Cohens and transferred by road to Stanningley, near Leeds, where she was scrapped at their yard. Somehow, her nameplates survived and in 1954 were discovered there and rescued by the Narrow Gauge Railway Society (and loaned to the Narrow Gauge Railway Museum at Tywyn in Wales). E.R. Calthrop was officially withdrawn on 31 December 1936 whilst stored under a tarpaulin at Waterhouses. The following February, Cohens used her for their demolition train, purchased her in May and cut her up at Waterhouses that October. Her nameplates too survived with one passing into private ownership and the other, the property of the Railway Club, also going on show at Tywyn. Her headlamp is now in the National Railway Museum at York.

The principal dimensions of the engines were:

Wheel diameter: driving	2ft 6in
: leading	1ft 11in
: trailing	1ft 11in
Wheelbase: coupled	6ft
: bogie	4ft
: total	20ft 6in
Boiler: diameter	3ft
: working pressure	150lb/sq.in
Heating surface: tubes (81)	363sq.ft
: firebox	42sq.ft
: total	405sq.ft
Cylinders: diameter	11½in
: stroke	16in
Grate area	10sq ft
Tank capacity	600 gal
Coal capacity (before increase)	1 ton
Weight in running order	26 tons 16cwt
Overall length	26ft 3in
Overall height	9ft 10in

Tractive effort of these locomotives has been given in the past as both 8,963lb and 9,790lb.

No.2 at Hulme End on 29 April 1933. *H.C. Casserley*

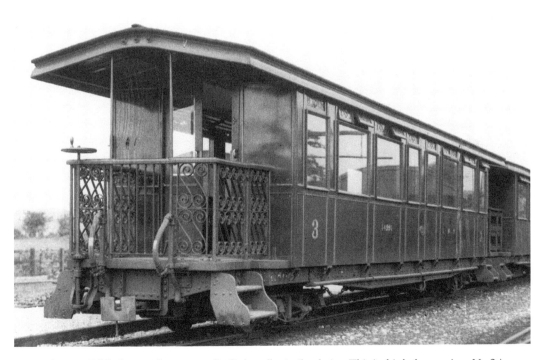

The Manifold's four carriages were all of a broadly similar design. This is third-class carriage No.2 in May 1934, now in LMS livery as 14991. *H.C. Casserley*

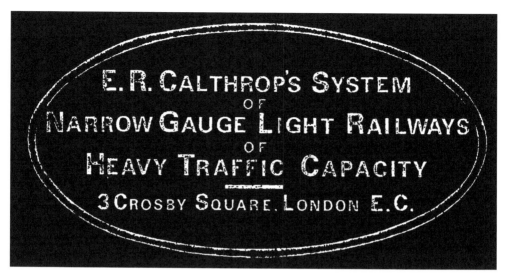

Copy of a Manifold rolling-stock plate proclaiming that the vehicle bearing it was designed by Calthrop.

The Coaches

Throughout its life the Manifold only possessed four passenger carriages – a number reflecting the sparsely-populated nature of the valley through which it ran – though, as will be seen, almost all of the railway's freight vehicles could be pressed into passenger service if the need arose. Designed by Calthrop, all four coaches were built for the line by the Electric Railway & Tramway Carriage Works Ltd and were bogie vehicles of the same basic design, the principal difference between them being that Nos 1 and 3 were first/third composites with a guard's compartment, and Nos 2 and 4 were third class only, divided into smoking and non-smoking sections.

Internally, seating was on cushioned transverse (single and double) and longitudinal (double) seats either side of a central aisle; the thirds held forty passengers and the composites eight first class (in individual armchairs) and thirty third class. The third-class compartments had seats upholstered in cloth, and flooring of wooden slats whilst the first-class portions sported buttoned leather and linoleum. Side luggage racks were also provided.

By all accounts the coaches were extremely comfortable (apart from their lack of heating), rode extremely well and were, considering their gauge, extremely spacious into the bargain – justification, indeed, of Calthrop's insistence on a wide loading gauge and a high standard of permanent way. Just how spacious they were is revealed by a report in the *Engineer* of 21 October 1904 stating that, on occasion, the coaches had carried over eighty passengers each! A rough and ready rule of thumb for the maximum safe width of narrow gauge stock is that it can be up to three times the width of the track gauge, and Calthrop took this to the limit – as the accompanying cross-section diagram shows – for which he had to obtain special Board of Trade sanction.

Externally the coaches were plainly of light railway or tramway appearance and displayed several noticeable features common to such vehicles on other British lines, with low-slung steps for boarding denoting the use of characteristic low-level 'platforms'. The roof, however, instead of having a conventional camber, sloped down on each side from a central ridge whilst the most distinctive visual feature, without any doubt, was the provision of canopied platforms, or verandahs, at each end of the thirds and at the first-class end of the composites. Enclosed to waist height with highly ornamental wrought-iron railings, these were very popular with passengers who were permitted to ride on them whilst the train was in motion. They also provided a means of access into the coaches (the third class section of the composites was gained via recessed side doors at the opposite end of the carriage, leading into the guard's compartment). As mentioned above, heating was non-existent apart from a stove in the guard's compartment, though all four carriages were equipped with Stone's patent (battery) electric lighting, the lamps being fitted with small, ornamental glass shades.

The coaches' underframes were of plate and angle iron, carried on diamond-frame swing-bolster bogies fitted with double laminated springs. The disc wheels were supplied by the British Griffin Chilled Iron & Steel Co. of Barrow-in-Furness. No buffers were fitted since their function was served by the central Jones-Calthrop patent coupler which was moved by radiating gear on the bogie so that it always engaged with that of another vehicle irrespective of whether they were on a curved or a straight section of track. Hand-brake wheels were provided on each verandah, and in the guards' compartments, though the main braking system relied on vacuum brakes supplied by the Automatic Vacuum Brake Co., the carriages being linked by two flexible pipes, one each side of the coupler so as to enable one at least to reach the much shorter pipes on the transporter wagons (the provision of two pipes at the end of the coaches has given rise, in the past, to the erroneous supposition that the vehicles were fitted with steam heating apparatus).

All in all, the vehicles were a most attractive sight, and their overall attractiveness was enhanced by their original primrose yellow livery, lined out in black, with the class numbers and the legend L&MVLtRly in a richly-decorated black script emblazoned twice on each side of the thirds and once on the sides of the composites (the coach number, in white, was carried on the chassis side frames). Roofs were painted white and the underframes and ironwork black. Sadly, this eye-catching colour scheme was changed by the NSR to match the new madder-lake livery applied to the locomotives, and was succeeded after the Grouping by LMS crimson lake, fully lined-out in black and yellow, again like the locomotives. An additional feature of LMS days

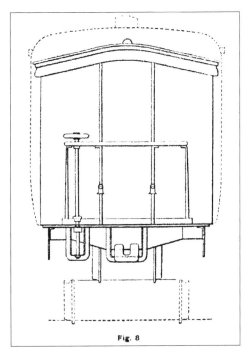

A diagram from the *Engineer* of 21 October 1904, showing an outline end view of one of the Manifold coaches (solid line) superimposed upon the end outline of an NSR horse-box (broken line), that railway's vehicle with the largest cross-sectional dimensions. The negligible difference in widths meant that Calthrop had designed the most spacious narrow gauge carriages in the British Isles.

Fig. 8

was a coach number painted on the sides – 14989 and 14990 for the composites and 14991 and 14992 for the thirds, with the initials LMS added in shaded letters.

After the closure of the line, the coaches stood at Waterhouses until burnt early in 1936 and their metalwork taken for scrap – the all-too common fate of withdrawn railway carriages and tramcars when no buyer could be found for them. Their principal dimensions are given below:

Length: over couplers	45ft
: over roof	43ft 6in
: over headstocks	42ft 10in
Width: overall	8ft
: over body	7ft 3in
: over underframe	7ft 2in
: inside	6ft 9in
Height: rail level to roof	9ft 9in
: floor to underside of roof	7ft 1in
Clear headroom (minimum)	6ft 3in
Wheel diameter	1ft 11in
Bogies: rigid wheelbase	4ft 3in
: centre to centre	28ft
Height of couplers above rail	1ft 2in (loaded)
Width of seats: 1st class	2ft 2in
: 3rd class	1ft 8in
Window size: 1st class	4ft 8in x 2ft 6in
: 3rd class	3ft 10in x 2ft 6in
Weight (3rds)	12 tons 14cwt

In the words of the *Locomotive Magazine* of 15 July 1904:

This rolling stock would appear to be of an abnormal size for a railway of only 2ft 6in gauge, but experience in India and the West Indies has proved after seven years' work that it is absolutely safe. Whatever doubts

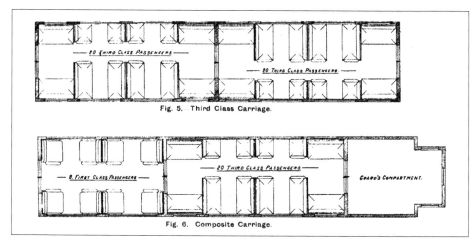

Plan views of the seat arrangements in both the third class and the composite carriages, from the *Tramway and Railway World* issue of 14 July 1904. (The vehicle's end balconies have been omitted.)

Nos 1 and 2, the Manifold's pair of low wagons, at Waterhouses. The railway's sole covered wagon, No.3, had the same underframe and running gear with an added body.

End-on view of a standard gauge wagon on a transporter (LMS 195313) at Hulme End. The hinged rails on the side platforms, added late in the vehicle's life so that it could carry milk tank wagons, are here folded down. Far left another wagon stands on a length of standard gauge track. *H.C. Casserley*

anyone may have as to the stability of these coaches, can be immediately dispelled by riding in them; they travel most smoothly, without any vibration or roll. Before the opening ceremony these coaches were tested at a speed of 30mph over the entire railway.

The Goods Stock

The Manifold's goods stock total never stood higher than eight – an astonishingly low figure in comparison with other British narrow gauge lines: the Welshpool & Llanfair Light Railway for example, which opened in 1903 and also relied primarily on agricultural traffic, possessed more than sixty wagons of various kinds (but only three coaches!). It should be remembered though that, whereas freight traffic was the main reason for the Manifold's existence, it was of a very compact nature: milk.

The eight vehicles fall neatly into three groups: the low wagons, the covered van and the transporters. Like the coaches, all were bogie vehicles fitted with both hand and vacuum brakes, and Jones-Calthrop patent couplers. Original livery was NSR red oxide, altered by the LMS to its own plain wagon grey. (It is probable that, in accordance with common rolling-stock manufacturing practice, some if not all of the freight vehicles were in a plain grey undercoat when delivered, and given their final coats of paint upon arrival.)

Nos 1 & 2, the low wagons

These two identical wagons were built for the railway by the Leeds Forge Co. Ltd at a cost of £225 each, and were virtually identical copies of ones designed by Calthrop in 1896 for the Barsi Light Railway. A special feature was the use of Fox's patent steel frames and bogies, and upon this underframe was mounted a very low body with high ends. The wagons were used principally for carrying milk churns though, if the need arose – usually at peak holiday times – portable knifeboard seats, iron hoops and canvas canopies could be added to turn them into very makeshift open carriages. (As mentioned earlier, they were so pressed into temporary passenger service on the opening day, with each on that occasion simply carrying two Manifold station seats, side by side, set back slightly from the centre line.) At some time late on in their life side steps were added, as if this aid to passengers was very much an afterthought!

At the Grouping the wagons were renumbered 195317 and 195318 by the LMS and they remained on the line until the very end; after being stored at Waterhouses they were then used on the 1937 demolition train before being scrapped that October. Their principal dimensions were:

Length: over couplers	28ft
: over floor	25ft
Width	7ft
Height of ends	6ft
Wheel diameter	1ft 11in
Bogies: rigid wheelbase	4ft 3in
: centre to centre	15ft 6in
Height of couplers above rail	1ft 2in (loaded)
Floor area	175sq. ft
Weight	5 tons 6cwt 1qr
Load (permitted)	14 tons 13cwt 3qr

No.3, the van

The railway's sole covered goods vehicle was also built by the Leeds Forge Co. Ltd and was basically the same low wagon underframe, bogies and running gear carrying a steel van body fitted with centre doors and end vents; in later years louvres for ventilation were added on each side of the doors. It, too, was principally used for milk runs (never for passengers) and was scrapped after storage at Waterhouses following the closure of the line. Its LMS number was 195316. Width was 5ft 6in and the height 9ft 6in to the top of its rounded roof; the other principal dimensions being as for the low wagons. It also could carry a load close to 15 tons, thus keeping the axle weighting below Calthrop's limit of 5 tons.

The transporters

These vehicles were perhaps the Manifold's most famous operating feature and their use has already been described. Two were ordered in April 1903 from Cravens Railway Carriage & Wagon Co. Ltd of Darnall, Sheffield, at a cost of £449 each, and at least one had arrived in time for the railway's grand opening. Towards the end of 1906 a further pair were ordered from the same builder, this time at a cost of only £315 each, and it is believed these were delivered a little over a year later.

All four of these original transporters were constructed to the same Calthrop design, the general principle of which can be easily grasped from photographs of them in use. Each vehicle was little more than a flat steel body with an 18in-wide platform, positioned 10in above the top of the rails, jutting out each side. In each platform (or, perhaps more correctly, shelf) was a groove which took the flange of a standard gauge wagon wheel; the standard gauge wheels themselves were secured with screw wedges to prevent movement once in place on the platforms. Loading and unloading were carried out in special docks where the two gauges met head-on, the larger vehicle simply being rolled or winched on or off the smaller one. This design meant that the usual type of upright brake pipe could not be used, so instead a short, horizontal pipe that did not impede the passage of the standard gauge wagons was fitted at each end, hence the provision of two pipes on the passenger vehicles so that coupling with the short pipe was assured.

In 1918 tests were run carrying loaded milk vans, the result being that one of the transporters was taken to Stoke and lengthened to enable it to take a standard NSR six-wheel milk van. This transporter later took the LMS number 195314; the other three were numbered 195311-13. Shortly after the Grouping the LMS delivered a fifth transporter, 195315, which had been built by the NSR at Stoke to the original, short, design.

Like the open wagons, the transporters could also be fitted with temporary seats for holiday traffic. These were benches made of angle-irons bent to a rough L shape and fitted with oak slats to form backs and seats; four would be bolted together to form a knifeboard seat running the length of the wagon, and a makeshift canvas awning erected to provide some degree of weather protection. The only other modification made to the transporters was the fitting in later years of hinged angle-irons on the side platforms that could take the wheels of rail milk tankers (instead of them running in the grooves), thereby raising the tankers the vital few inches needed for their comparatively low-slung brake gear to clear the main body of the transporters.

The transporters' last task on the Manifold was to serve on the demolition train, carrying standard gauge wagons laden with the footpath materials as well as removing the lifted rails. Their work over, all except No.195312 were cut up at Waterhouses, the survivor being sold in 1935 to the Clay Cross Co. of Derbyshire, the owner of the Ashover Light Railway. The price was £35 plus £6 17s (£6.85) for delivery. There it was converted to 60cm (nominal 2ft) gauge but a trial run showed that it would not prove possible to use it to convey coal wagons over the line as intended, the principal reason being that since that railway had not been laid to the Manifold's permanent way standards, the transporter's bogies fouled its own framing on the Ashover's tight curves. Consequently it stood, unused, until scrapped in 1951 following the closure of the railway.

The transporters' principal dimensions were:

	Short	Long
Length over headstocks	19ft 6in	31ft
Overall width	8ft	8ft
Wheel diameter	1ft 9in	1ft 9in
Bogies: rigid wheelbase	4ft 3in	4ft 3in
: centre to centre	9ft	20ft
Height of coupling (loaded)	1ft 2in	1ft 2in

Unfortunately, figures given in the past for the weights of these vehicles do not agree but it would seem that the original transporters weighed about 4¾ tons and the lengthened version correspondingly more. Curiously, early accounts state that each could carry a load of 20 tons which, if true, would have resulted in an axle load of over 6 tons – well in excess of Calthrop's limit.

Visitors

As mentioned earlier, trials were undertaken on the Manifold in July 1932 with the chassis of an Armstrong-Whitworth diesel-electric railcar, built in Newcastle-upon-Tyne for the 2ft 6in gauge Gaekwar of Baroda's State Railway in India. Part of an order of four, this vehicle had a 6-cylinder Armstrong-Sawer engine, mounted at one end above a 6-wheel bogie, providing 98hp at 2,000rpm to a generator. A single electric motor, centrally-mounted below the chassis, drove a fixed pair of driving wheels at the other end of the vehicle.

Interestingly, this was not the first time the Manifold had been used for trials of stock destined for the sub-continent. Before it was sent out for service on the 2ft 6in gauge Kalka-Simla Railway in northern India in June 1921, the chassis of an early diesel-mechanical railcar was tested on the line. Built by Baguley Cars Ltd of Burton-upon-Trent (for the Drewery Car Co.) as works number 903, and some 18ft long and 7ft wide, this was a 2-4-2 chassis with a coupled wheelbase of 4ft 6in and an overall wheelbase of 12ft. It was powered by a 6-cylinder Baguley engine rated at 45/50hp, with a 3-speed gearbox and silent chain drive to one axle; it was fitted before export with an unusual, open but roofed body somewhat reminiscent of that of a charabanc, in that it was single-ended with the rear seats raised to afford passengers a clearer view ahead, and was accompanied to India by a twin vehicle, works number 904.

In 1927 the same firm constructed a similar vehicle for the same railway. Works number 1625, this was rated at 80hp and again had four coupled drivers but this time only two carrying wheels; again, the chassis was tested on the Manifold. The trials of these two designs, with seating for sixteen and fourteen passengers respectively, were separated by the testing in 1923 of another 'visitor', Baguley works number 1320, a massive forty-three-seater 60hp 0-4-4 destined for the Barbados Government Railways.

Finally, it should be noted that as early as 1906, a Drewry four-seater railcar was tested on the line. Details are sketchy but, being of only 6hp, it would not have been of any real use for public service and the supposition is that it was considered for purchase as an inspection car, or a very lightweight 'directors' saloon'. In the event, its purchase was rejected but, as it transpired, it proved to be merely the first in a succession of similar but more advanced vehicles to visit the railway.

Other stock

As noted earlier, two steam locomotives were used by Lovatts during the Manifold's construction, these being *Skylark* on the northern section and *Sirdar* – the name is a Persian term for a military commander - on the southern. *Skylark* was an outside-framed 0-4-2 side tank, with 7 ½in x 12in outside cylinders and 2ft 3in diameter coupled wheels, built by Kerr, Stuart & Co. Ltd of Stoke-upon-Trent in 1903 (works number 802) whilst *Sirdar* was a smaller 0-4-0 tank, with 6in x 10in outside cylinders and 2ft wheels, from the same builders (works number 749 of 1902). Both were built to order for the purpose of working on the Manifold contract.

Sometime after construction finished the two locomotives were possibly used on other contracts, or else lay idle, before being sold on a few years later. At the outbreak of the First World War both were bought by the Admiralty, from a dealer, for dockyard use and both went to Kent, with *Skylark* going to Ridham Dockyard on the Swale, just north of Sittingbourne, and *Sirdar* to (it is believed) Hoo Ness – both 2ft 6in gauge systems. After the war, the two were put up for sale as surplus to requirements and, in 1922, *Skylark*, having been purchased from another dealer, resurfaced on the Snailbeach District Railways. This grandly-named Shropshire system was in fact a short mineral railway linking the lead mines at Snailbeach with the national railway system at Pontesbury near Shrewsbury. Here – minus its name – it took the number 2 and, after re-gauging to 2ft 4in, worked through until the railway's closure in 1947 before being scrapped three years later. The post-First World War history of *Sirdar* is unknown.

Lastly, details of an intriguing 'what might have been' deserve inclusion here. According to Robin Barnes, writing in the October 1986 issue of *Railway World*, someone in the LMS's drawing office at Derby is believed to have designed, in 1930, a small 2-4-2 tank engine for use on the Manifold, to which one can only say: 'If so, why?' Perhaps it was just the result of a bored draughtsman indulging in an afternoon flight of fancy... but then, as it was the Manifold, who could blame him?

six
Afterlife

A Walk Down the Line

Today, more than seventy years after its closure, what remains of the Manifold railway for the visitor to the valley to discover? The answer is that although most of the line's associated buildings, and all of the track, have gone, virtually the whole of the railway's track bed is there to be walked or cycled over. The only snag is that if you choose to do the whole walk, you will need to arrange transport from the other end unless you intend making the return journey under your own steam! Since so many of the station features have vanished, taking a good guidebook to the railway and/or valley is a must for correct identification of their sites.

The Manifold Track – as it is officially known – begins at the railway's former southern terminus, in the middle of the village of Waterhouses, beside the A523 Leek-Ashbourne road. A signpost indicates to visitors the turning to take off the main road, under the old standard gauge railway bridge and up into the car park laid out on the site of the goods yard. The railway's sole surviving structure here is the former goods shed, now housing a bicycle-hire business, beside which is somewhat incongruously sited an otherwise excellent block of public conveniences. From here on there is no need of signposts as the only path to take leads the walker along the terrace formerly occupied by the standard gauge tracks high above the main road. Passing a monument erected in 1977 to commemorate the Queen's Silver Jubilee, the site of the former Waterhouses Station is reached. Recognition of what once stood here is almost impossible, for much of the site – including the narrow gauge bridge just west of the platforms – was physically removed in the mid-1960s when the main road was widened. An overgrown path descends eastwards to join the pavement by the road, which it follows until the site of the former level crossing is reached. Here the Manifold track bed proper, now with a tarmac surface, begins.

Immediately over the A523 the track crosses the first of the many river bridges it will encounter on its journey to Hulme End, and the falling gradient of the route is readily apparent – as is the luxuriant growth of trees and other vegetation alongside the path, providing a marked contrast to the scene shown in photographs of the railway years. Indeed, this natural encroachment, more than anything else, indicates just how much time has passed since the last train ran. The path itself is about 6ft wide, well surfaced and fenced on both sides; the distances between the fences, and the broad sweep of its curves, show how generously the railway was laid out, and it is difficult to believe that here was but a single narrow gauge track. The fences are modern but some of the gates – notably the kissing gates with their upright wooden bars – were there when the trains ran.

After the path reaches the site of Sparrowlee station, where the raised siding can just about be made out, the valley begins to close in and the crossing and re-crossing of the (usually dry) Hamps become more frequent. Some of the bridges are as they were left after the closure but others have had their wooden sleeper decks replaced by concrete. This is the longest stretch (two miles) between stations and, walking it, one cannot but reflect what a superb setting it was for an unhurried train journey (and very reminiscent of the lower stretches of the Corris Railway,

Afterlife: comparing photographs of the railway's remains with those of it when alive shows just how much has changed at Waterhouses – and just how little elsewhere. This was the former goods yard at Waterhouses in 1979, with the goods shed now joined by a block of toilets.

Looking back to the goods shed from the site of the station, 1979. The unattractive 'monument' was erected in 1977 to commemorate the Queen's Silver Jubilee. The shed now houses a bicycle-hire business for the benefit of anyone wishing to explore the Hamps and Manifold valleys and the whole area has since been landscaped rather more attractively.

The site of the former level crossing over the Ashbourne road in 1979, the point where the Manifold Track leaves the roadway – a scene much the same today.

or parts of the Welshpool & Llanfair Light Railway, in Wales). Quite abruptly, at Beeston Tor, the way ahead is blocked by the looming hillside of that name, while in from the left 'runs' the (usually equally-dry) River Manifold. Close by in a meadow still stands the railway's wooden refreshment room, now a very dilapidated structure. After the railway closed it was used for a time as a summer camping house, then became a farmer's storehouse.

A metalled path (Earl Cathcart's Road) from the lower Manifold Valley parallels the track bed to Grindon station. Here, at four miles from Waterhouses – roughly halfway along the path – the first real contact with the outside world is made with the level crossing of the Wetton-Grindon minor road by Weags Bridge. Anyone caring to branch off on this will quickly realise how far any centres of population – or indeed any houses at all – were from the railway, and what an effort had to be made to climb from the very floor of the valley to the very top in order to reach them! Small wonder then that the Manifold's local passenger traffic was almost non-existent for most of its life.

The former siding at Grindon is now a car park and, from here on, the path becomes increasingly frequented by visitors as the vistas become more delightful. The next station site is that of Thor's Cave, overshadowed by the slightly unreal spectacle of that huge cave mouth gaping blackly in the 300ft cliff (and reached by a steep scramble); here, as at most of the stations, the remains of foundations and platform can still be made out by a searching eye (one clue is that on the roadway section of the path, the former siding side of the stations provides parking space for cars).

Midway between Thor's Cave and Wetton Mill comes Redhurst Crossing, by the crossing over the Wetton-Butterton minor road; the River Manifold is also crossed here for the first time and the path, a little wider now, is open to motor vehicles. Wetton Mill has developed into the main centre from which to explore the middle section of the line and the former station site is now a long car park, while the attractive cluster of mill buildings just across the river includes a small but welcome tea-room. The river here is decidedly wet, for it is a short way below the mill that it disappears down its swallet holes where a number of curious relics from the turn of the last

Recurrent, substantial reminders of the former railway are the many bridges adapted for their new role. This is the one over the (usually dry) River Manifold at Redhurst Crossing, as it was in 1979.

century can be seen: in an effort to keep the Manifold flowing on the surface Sir Thomas Wardle had these swallets blocked with concrete but, alas, the air pressure in the underground passages built up to such an extent that the seals were blown clean out! Attempts to relieve the pressure by sinking iron pipes failed and the assorted junk was left to baffle future visitors.

Northwards from Wetton Mill the track bed remains open to cars as far as Butterton and, as they pass through Swainsley Tunnel, a perculiar, resonant, booming noise is produced by the echo. On foot, one is struck by the sheer size of the structure for a narrow gauge line – a forcible reminder of Calthrop's advocation of transporter wagons and the consequent need for an outsize loading gauge. Clearly visible are the staggered shelter recesses (three per side) and the remains of the whitewash that once coated the walls. Since whitewashing the interiors of tunnels is not standard railway practice, it is thought that this was done to help illuminate the tunnel during the Second World War, when it was commandeered by the army and used as an ammunition store complete with sandbagged portals and armed sentries. Electric lights now keep it permanently lit as an aid to drivers. Immediately upon leaving the tunnel, the roadway turns sharply right whilst the path (and track bed) carries straight on over the Warslow Brook to the site of Butterton station. The concrete foundations of the station building here were removed in the winter of 1952-1953, apparently the last of such remains on the line to be obliterated with any other survivors left to become overgrown in peace.

Half a mile further on comes Ecton, once the scene of so much activity on and beside the railway, but now little more than a couple of overgrown embankments, a derelict building or two and arid expanses of stony wasteland. The creamery has gone and the quarry workings which scar the hillside are slowly being reclaimed by nature. Beyond here the valley begins to open out and the path makes its way over the final stretch to Hulme End. About a quarter of a mile out from the terminus was one of the railway's tightest curves and it is a decidedly strange sensation to walk the path here as it faithfully reproduces the former cant of the track. By the time Hulme

The Wetton Mill complex of buildings, also little changed over the years, as seen from the river bridge on a summer evening in 2002. The bridge was built by the Duke of Devonshire in 1807 to replace one washed away by floods. *Jan Dobrzynski*

End is reached by way of one of the railway's few embankments and occupation bridges, the sense of being enclosed in a valley has completely gone.

Hulme End is a far smaller village than Waterhouses, and one has to marvel at the sheer optimism of the Manifold's promoters in expecting any passenger traffic from here at all. But for that optimism, and for what it has left us, we can only give thanks – for what it has left us is the whole station site virtually intact. True, the carriage shed has gone but the engine shed remains – and, wonder of wonders, so does the original wooden station building. In 1989, after seriously considering moving it elsewhere, Staffordshire County Council began a long-term project centred on this structure, with its exterior renovation (included a new roof and a new platform canopy to replace the long-vanished original) completed in the summer of 1995 before attention then turned to its interior. The next two years saw this task tackled, plus the landscaping of much of the adjoining land, to convert the station into a (manned) Visitor Centre with an adjoining picnic area. Financial support for the scheme came from the EC, the Peak District National Park Authority, the Rural Development Commission and the local authority of the time, the Staffordshire Moorlands Peak District Council. The refurbished building was officially opened on 26 August 1997 by the Chairman of the Council, Councillor Mrs Jocelyn Finn, and the MEP for Peak District, Arlene McCarthy. Inside the building are displays concentrating on the Manifold Valley and its railway, whilst outside on the 'platform' rebuilt station seats supply an extra touch of realism. Finally, August 2009 saw the opening of the (completely rebuilt) engine shed as the Tea Junction café. On a hot summer's day, with eyes closed, one can almost hear a train whistle echoing somewhere down the valley...

The Manifold's northern terminus, again in 1979: the embankment approach, complete with a bridge allowing cattle to pass under the track bed from one field to another...

Keeping the memory alive

For the narrow gauge enthusiast, no British line can be truly dead whilst its memory is kept alive and, even though the Manifold belonged to a world irrevocably altered by the historical events and social changes of the last sixty years or more, interest in it has never been stronger. Collectors are willing to pay spiralling prices for items associated with the railway, while modellers are catered for with ever-increasing numbers of locomotive, carriage and wagon kits produced in a wide range of scales.

Moving up in size somewhat from model to miniature railways, the Manifold has been reborn in this guise as well. A project to recapture some of the old railway's atmosphere with a live steam miniature line reached fruition when, on 27 June 1978, a 10¼in gauge railway, half a mile in length, was opened on the old NSR track bed between Rudyard Lake and Rudyard stations on the former Macclesfield-Cheddleton Junction line just north of Leek. Operated and built by the Leek & Manifold Valley Light Railway Co. Ltd in the form of Headmaster Brian Nicholson and pupils of Waterhouses School, the open carriages were hauled by No.1 *E.R. Calthrop*, built 1974 by Coleby-Simkins Engineering Ltd of Melton Mowbray as a one-third scale model of the Manifold's original No.1. (The line was dismantled in 1980 with the present-day, non-Manifold-themed railway opening on the site five years later.)

Taking its cue from this development, the first edition of this book closed with the words: 'The spirit and the memory of the Manifold most definitely live on, but could it be that once again the sounds of steam, albeit on a smaller scale, might be heard in the Manifold Valley?' Just a few years later, the answer to that question was a resounding 'Yes!' In the 1980s a small band of dedicated individuals succeeded in obtaining permission to operate a 10¼in gauge miniature steam railway on the actual former track bed of the Manifold, albeit as an annual temporary

... the site in use as a Highways Department yard...

event. Using volunteers, with much of the labour performed by employees of Belle Engineering of nearby Sheen, a temporary track would be laid alongside the footpath south from Hulme End station. On this, during three summer weekends (usually the last three in June), a one-third scale model of *J.B. Earle*, built by Doug Blackhurst, would haul a handful of yellow open coaches full of fare-paying passengers, the proceeds going to Cancer Relief. By 1988 the track had extended some three quarters of a mile to a terminus named Apes Tor for Ecton, about a mile short of Swainsley Tunnel. Accompanying the railway operation was a visitors' exhibition on display in the station building at Hulme End.

It would seem a truism to say that every British narrow gauge railway will, at some time after its demise, give rise to an organised group dedicated to preserving its memory. The Manifold has been no exception to this rule and, as a result of interest generated by the Steam Weekends at Hulme End, the Manifold Valley Light Railway Society was born at an inaugural meeting held on Monday 20 July 1987 at the Minton House Hotel, Hartington. As stated in the very first issue of its magazine and newsletter, the *Manifold Valley Echo*, the Society's aims were simple:

To bring together all those with a common interest in the Leek and Manifold Valley Light Railway and the area and community it served.
To take all necessary steps to ensure the memory, traditions and spirit of the LMVLR live on by historical research and recording of information.
Where possible, maintaining whatever is still evident.
To act as a co-ordinating body to all those responsible authorities in the area.

The Society's Honorary Chairman was Dr J.R. Hollick – now sadly now longer with us – the acknowledged expert on the Manifold, and a member of the 'MANIFOLD' consortium responsible for the first definitive histories of the NSR and the Manifold (see Bibliography & Sources).

... and the surviving station building and loco shed, from the opposite vantage point.

Interestingly, no mention was made in its aims of attempting to rebuild even part of the railway, and this alone set the Society apart from virtually every other group of its kind: the emphasis was very much on the preservation of what survived, not the replacement – or even the replication – of the old Manifold with locomotives and stock from elsewhere. This was preservation in its truest sense, not the loose definition of the word adopted by some 'preserved' railways. To this end the Society lobbied and negotiated for the restoration of the station building at Hulme End and, as recounted above, did so successfully. This achieved, and the future of the railway's other remains in the valley assured, it quietly disbanded.

Outside the valley, the Manifold preservation story continues, the latest turn of which concerns the Waterhouses signal box. After the closure of the station to all traffic, the site was cleared (with the exception of the goods shed, already noted) but, miraculously, the wooden signal box somehow also escaped burning and was sold to become an outbuilding on a farm at Throwley, near Ilam (the nameboard was rescued and is now in the National Railway Museum at York). Then, in the early 1990s, the signal box was moved to the Rectory at Wetton where it languished – though virtually intact, with its glazing, slates and roof finials – before being acquired by the volunteer-operated 2ft gauge Amerton Railway at Stowe-by-Chartley, six miles north-east of Stafford. It was moved there by low-loader on 8 August 2001 to be restored, sympathetically, to house the railway's existing ground frame so that it can once again do the job it was (at least partly) built for: controlling operations on a Staffordshire narrow gauge railway.

Beside buildings and track-bed, a number of other physical relics of the Manifold survive in museums and private collections. Like any railway, the Manifold generated a good deal of ephemera such as timetables, posters, tickets and the like, all of which are sought keenly by collectors; examples can also be found in local and national museums, along with more substantial items such as the loco relics mentioned earlier and a station bench, with new wood on old iron legs said to be from Wetton Mill, in the Narrow Gauge Railway Museum at Tywyn.

There this account of the Manifold comes to a natural end – for the present at least, for who can say what further turns the story will take in the future? Although it seems unlikely – certainly in the short to medium term – that even a part of the railway will ever be rebuilt in anything like its original form, a flavour of what a journey on it might have been like can be tasted on a visit to its Welsh contemporary, the Welshpool & Llanfair Light Railway, whose history so often complemented that of the Manifold. After losing its passenger services in 1931 this railway survived – in contrast to its Staffordshire counterpart – as a goods-only line until 1956, when it was closed by its then owners, British Railways. In 1963, however, part of it re-opened to the public with operation by a preservation society, since when virtually the whole of the original railway has been rebuilt. In this part of rural Britain, at least, one can stand on the end verandah of a 2ft 6in gauge saloon carriage as it trundles along, through glorious farming countryside, behind a century-old tank engine.

On the Manifold, the journey has to be made in the imagination. Perhaps, with all the original stock destroyed, and the valley's sleepy way of life changed for ever, that is for the best.

In contrast a replica bench on the platform, outside the refurbished station building in 2002, looking for all the world as though it has always been here... *Jan Dobrzynski*

... at the end of the line. *Jan Dobrzynski*

Journey's end for many explorers of the 'secret valley', now as then: the Manifold Inn – formerly the Light Railway Hotel – at Hulme End.

Looking south to Thor's Cave, from the site of the station of that name.

Swainsley Tunnel: the south portal.

Hulme End station building and original engine shed from across the picnic area, once the goods yard.

A closer view of the renovated station building, now a visitors' centre. *Jan Dobrzynski*

Bibliography & Sources

Earlier histories of the Manifold and the NSR are:

Christiansen, Rex & Miller, R.W. *The North Staffordshire Railway*, David & Charles 1971
    0715351214
Jenkins, Stanley C. *The Leek and Manifold Light Railway*, Locomotion Paper No. 179
    The Oakwood Press 1991 0853614148
'Manifold' The Leek & Manifold Valley Light Railway, J.H. Henstock Ltd, Ashbourne 1955
 – *The North Staffordshire Railway*, J.H. Henstock Ltd, Ashbourne 1952
Turner, Keith *The Leek & Manifold Valley Light Railway*, David & Charles 1980 071537950X

Excellent and comprehensive video coverage of the Manifold, including archive film footage and still photographs, can be found on:

Cartwright, Robin *The Leek and Manifold Valley Light Railway*
– *Part 1 1896-1904*, Robert Cartwright Productions, Stafford 1992 9999003451
– *Part 2 1904-1934,* Audio Visual Services, Stafford 1992 999900346X
– *Part 3 The Heyday of the Railway*, Cartwright Visual Services, Stafford 1993
    9999003443

The wide range of background material drawn upon for this study includes numerous journals, maps, guide books, local histories, directories and yearbooks, as well as general railway histories and reference works.

Principal printed sources consulted, as well as official documents, have been cited in the text.

DESIGNED AND ERECTED
BY THE
PORTABLE BUILDING Co Ltd
FLEETWOOD
& AT MANCHESTER LONDON
& JOHANNESBURG SOUTH AFRICA

Brass plate fixed to Hulme End
Station building.

Acknowledgements

I should like to express my gratitude and appreciation to everyone who has been kind enough to assist me, over many years, during the research into the story of the Manifold. They include Harold W. Butcher, Jan Dobrzynski, H.C. Casserley, Richard Casserley, Dr Patrick J. Cossey, Robert Keys, David R. Morgan, Brian Nicholson, Paul Smith, Jack Tempest, Peter Treloar and the staff of Birmingham City Library, Cambridge University Library, Leek Library and the National Railway Museum, as well as the Librarian and other members of the Narrow Gauge Railway Society not named above.

Special thanks must go to Eric Leslie for permitting the use of his delightfully evocative drawings, to Margaret Donnison for the location map and gradient profile, and to G.V. Wingfield-Digby for allowing me to quote from his Journal.

Unless otherwise noted, photographic illustrations are by the author, or from the author's collection.

If you are interested in purchasing other books published by The History Press, or in case you have difficulty finding any of our books in your local bookshop, you can also place orders directly through our website
www.thehistorypress.co.uk